ALLOW ME
TO
INTRODUCE

An Insider's Guide
to the Occult

LON MILO DUQUETTE
FOREWORD BY BRANDY WILLIAMS

WEISER BOOKS

This edition first published in 2020 by Weiser Books,
an imprint of
Red Wheel/Weiser, LLC
With offices at:
65 Parker Street, Suite 7
Newburyport, MA 01950
www.redwheelweiser.com

ISBN: 978-1-57863-654-9
Library of Congress Cataloging-in-Publication Data
available upon request.

Cover design by Kathryn Sky-Peck
Cover photograph by Shutterstock
Interior by Steve Amarillo / Urban Design LLC
Typeset in Adobe Bembo and Trajan

Printed in the United States of America
IBI
10 9 8 7 6 5 4 3 2 1

ALLOW ME
TO
INTRODUCE

*This book is dedicated to my dear friend
and fellow baby-boomer troubadour, occultist,
writer, lecturer, musician, and magician,
Donald Michael Kraig*
(March 28, 1951–March 17, 2014).

CONTENTS

The author wishes to humbly thank his "lucky stars"—the immortal luminaries of the firmament of magical literature for whom it has been his honor and privilege to *introduce*.

FOREWORD

I am a woman, a priestess, and a magician. Being a priestess clearly means I am a woman priest. Being a magician and also a woman is less obvious. It's hard to find a teacher who can talk to a woman magician. I often feel treated as I am "other," "outside," struggling to read myself into the role.

Lon Milo DuQuette never makes me feel like that. I've always had the sense that he is talking directly to me, inviting me into the fascinating world of magic. His primary purpose as a teacher and a writer is not to display his knowledge (which is broad and deep) or his magical accomplishments (which are magnificent) but to open the door so that we can share that knowledge and have those experiences. He centers not on his own needs as teacher but on the needs of the student. He shares his knowledge without fuss, laying out study plans that don't skip steps or hold back secrets but instead make practice possible. His magic is not for himself only; he practices in order to share. As a writer, a teacher, and a magician, he is generous.

His great genius is to make magic accessible. The esoteric arts have built up over the centuries into bewildering layers of ideas and systems. The texts, when they are in English at all, are often written in an older form of the language. Just translating antique ideas into contemporary English is a service in itself. For example, with all deference to the prophet Aleister Crowley, his prose is as dense as Shakespeare. It needs an introduction, an explanation of the obscure phrases, a translator. Lon Milo DuQuette provides that translation.

This book is a collection of introductions and prefaces to books. In these pages, Enochian language, tarot, Qabbalah, geomancy, all seem like keys to understanding the universe and ourselves. It's clear these studies and practices have changed Lon's life and his delight shines on every page. Reading the books in this list would constitute a mighty magical education.

Lon excels at introducing other magicians. He is equally at home with long-dead masters of antiquity and the newest generation of innovators. He has known the most influential magickians of his lifetime and tells us he is profoundly grateful to the people who taught him. His mentors, Grady McMurtry and Phyllis Seckler and Israel Regardie, are among the people who trained directly with Aleister Crowley. They died in his lifetime; Lon is our bridge to that generation of Thelemites.

In these pages he tells the story of his initiation into Ordo Templi Orientis. As I have come to know Lon directly through my own membership in the order, I have come to deeply appreciate his lifetime of service. His tireless work has helped to build and shape O.T.O. into the worldwide magickal order it is today. When

Grady and Phyllis picked him to be their initiate they chose wisely, and we are the beneficiaries.

If you have a chance to attend one of his lectures or classes, jump at it! If you find that you are scheduled against one of his presentations, you might find your audience sparse indeed. He's a hard act to follow too. I was once offered a chance to present at a conference in his stead when he had to withdraw because of a conflict. I said "I'm honored that you thought of me and I'd love to do it. But . . . you know I'm not funny, right?" Lon is one of those genuinely wise people who also have the gift of humor. Being able to laugh is one of the keys to success, he says, especially if you can laugh at yourself.

These days Lon is as likely to give a concert as a lecture. From the fiery anthem "Class Warfare" to the searing indictment "If We Believed" to the crooning lullaby "Sweet Babalon" the audience sings along. He gives voice to the pains and fears and joys of a magical life. Music threads through this book, in liner notes for a musical presentation of the tarot, in an address to an audience about to hear Mozart's *The Magic Flute,* in the musicality of the prose.

In these introductions to other people's work we get to know Lon through the books and people he loves. He is exactly the right kind of guru—funny, kind, accessible, stern when severity is called for, and demanding that the students take responsibility for the learning. Hilarious anecdotes segue into breathtaking vistas of insight. He is speaking a lived revelation, singing the truth of the soul: the earth is sunlight incarnate, we are the earth's children, our embodiment is the call to spiritual awareness that we are all eternal.

The best description of Lon Milo DuQuette is his own description of Donald Michael Kraig.

In the final analysis, the only meaningful credential a magician can present to the world is the *magician*. Has he or she evolved through the agency of magic? Is he or she a wiser, more balanced, more disciplined, more enlightened, more engaged, more self-aware individual? Is the individual a better friend, a better teacher, a better citizen, a better human being because of his or her involvement in this most personal of spiritual art forms? Most importantly, does the magician have the ability to laugh at *magician*?

Lon Milo DuQuette is one of the greatest teachers of our time. In these introductions he shows us the magician that he is, demonstrating how to embody a magical life. He tells us that he writes the books he wanted to read. As a woman magician I too am writing the books I needed when I was starting out. I look to Lon as the exemplar of the writer as teacher; I could not have a better one.

Brandy Williams
author of *Practical Magic*

PREFACE

I'm a very lucky man. I've endured seventy-two years in relatively good health. I've always managed to reside with my family in a part of the universe that is warm, sunny, and relatively safe. I am blessed to be married to beautiful saint of a wife and father to a brilliant doctor of a son. Month-after-month, year-after-year I somehow scrape up the rent and put food on the table. The DuQuettes live modestly. We've never owned a house, a new car, or a credit card. Considering the fact that I am a bit of a bum, that I possess little ambition, have never made any long-term plans or set any life goals—I am happy as any human being deserves to be.

In 1950 I was *lucky* when that pain in my hip was Perthes bone disease and not polio.

In 1955, I was *lucky* to catch the first cultural wave of dawning rock 'n' roll and television.

In 1960 I was *lucky* to be given a guitar.

In 1965 I was *lucky* to become socially awakened and impelled to involve myself in the peace, and civil rights and social justice movements.

In 1966 I was *lucky* to be introduced to LSD and the subtle wisdom of the *I Ching* and the *Tao*, and the teachings of Lao Tzu and Buddha, Yogananda, Yogi Ramacharakra, Ramakrishna, Vivekananda, Alan Watts and Timothy Leary.

In 1967 I was *lucky* to become so prophetically "inspired" while on LSD that I telephoned Constance in Nebraska and proposed marriage. (I was profoundly *lucky* she said "Yes" (though she says the jury's still out whether or not she was lucky!)

In 1969 I was *lucky* to sign an artist/songwriter recording contract with Epic Records.

In 1971 I was *lucky* when I accidentally enrolled in the Lee Strasberg Theatre and Film Institute.[1]

In 1972 I was *lucky* to be amused and fascinated by writings of Aleister Crowley.

In 1975 I was *lucky* to meet and be initiated by the aging disciples of Crowley's magical orders and formally began my study and practice of Western Ceremonial Magick.

---

1 I had been waiting alone in the lobby of the studio while my friend auditioned. Suddenly, John Marley, the famed character actor, stuck his head out of a studio door and shouted, "Next!" "What the hell?" I thought and followed him into the bowels of the studio and he introduced me to another great character actor, Gerald S. O'Loughlin, who sat me down and asked me in his best tough New York police detective voice, "So! Why do you *wanna* be an *actah?*" "I don't want to be an actor." I said. "I just want to be truthful in living my own drama." I guess that was just the kind of answer a method acting school was looking for. I was accepted without having to audition.

In 1988 I received a phone call from one of my favorite contemporary authors, Christopher S. Hyatt, PhD. A year or so earlier I had initiated him into our local lodge of *Ordo Templi Orientis* in Newport Beach. He asked if I would care to contribute a chapter to his new book on Western Tantra.[2] I had never thought about writing anything professionally but it felt like something I might enjoy, so I said "Sure!" I borrowed a friend's word processor and wrote up a few words that I felt would be appropriate. In 1990 Dr. Hyatt called again and asked if I would be interested in co-authoring a book with him about the magical and qabalistic aspects of Tarot *vis-a-vis* his Jungian theories on the subject. I told him I was completely unqualified to comment authoritatively and suggested he try someone else. When he asked *who?* I was hard pressed to come up with the name of a *living* authority. It dawned on me in the years I had been blissfully studying and practicing this stuff most of my personal mentors had died.

I said, "Sure!" and for the next two years Dr. Hyatt and I would write four books together, and I would contribute to a handful of other books released by the same publisher. Since then, and for the last quarter century, I've enjoyed wonderful relationships with other fine publishers and have written a number of books on Magick, Tarot, Qabalah, Freemasonry, indeed, whatever subjects I might care to write about.

Over the years, it has been my good fortune to make the acquaintance of some of the most talented and important esoteric writers of my generation, some of whom, from time-to-time, have graciously invited

2   Christopher S. Hyatt, PhD, *Secrets of Western Tantra*. Scottsdale, Arizona: New Falcon Publications, 1989.

me to contribute introductions or forewords to their books. For me, this is a great honor and privilege. I take these opportunities very seriously because they oblige me to do my best to cut to the chase and distill my thoughts on any particular subject and do it as succinctly as possible. As a literary form, however, such introductory material is often skimmed over or ignored by the reader who is understandably anxious to get on to the meat of the text.

I was sad to think that these short writings would likely remain the most overlooked of all my works. So, I especially want to thank the various authors and publishers of the works represented here for allowing me to share them once again. As the various works span a broad range of magical subjects and decades of my own evolving understanding and opinions I have grouped the essays together in the broadest subject categories, fully expecting the reader not to feel obliged to read the essays in strict order but to jump around as interest and spirit moves. I am leaving it to the reader's wise use of the Contents page to navigate his or her way around.

PART ONE

TEACHERS, HEROES AND MENTORS

It isn't often life presents us with opportunities to properly express our gratitude and admiration to those individuals, teachers, heroes, and mentors, who for one reason or another have been directly responsible for shaping the quality of our character or the course of our life's trajectory. I can say without hesitation that Aleister Crowley (who died a few months before I was born) and Israel Regardie (who I had the pleasure of meeting and corresponding with) top my list of teachers, heroes, and mentors. I consider it an example of true magical *kismet* that my life circumstances have conspired to allow me to write about some of the very same works that inspired me in my youth; works that launched me on my fifty-year adventures in magick, writing, and teaching. I feel that it is profoundly appropriate that I begin this anthology of literary appetizers with my introductory words to several of the books that first introduced me to magick in general, and the works of Aleister Crowley in particular.

The Tree of Life

A Study in Magic

FOREWORD FOR THE 2017 EDITION[1]

But it is only man himself who may
tauten the string of the bow.

—ISRAEL REGARDIE

My life is Magick.[2] Ultimately, the same can be said of everyone's life for *magick* in the truest sense of the word is the mechanism of consciousness, and consciousness is the nature of existence itself. Such vaporous musing, however profound and accurate, is a rather obscure way to open a discussion on the theories and practices of modern occultism and not at all what someone is expecting to hear when they ask you, "What is Magick?"

Since the early 1970s when I was first exposed to it as a spiritual art form, magick in its many varieties has been my passion. This passion soon developed into practice; and mastering the practice continues to be for me an on-going adventure in self-transformation and self-realization. Magick is my "Way."

Gradually, over the years, I have been able to share my observations and commentaries on magical subjects in published platforms and (very late in life) these projects

---

1 Written for Israel Regardie, *The Tree of Life: A Study in Magic,* Scottsdale, Arizona: New Falcon Publications, 2017.
2 "Magic(k)" being a modern convention to distinguish the spiritual art form from stage "magic" or prestidigitation.

have earned for me a modest literary career. Frequently, in my capacity as a practitioner and commentator on the subject of magick, I have the opportunity to travel and discuss my books and hold workshops. Obviously, I am not a shy person, and on long flights, I enjoy talking to the people seated next to me on the plane and learning about their lives. They, in turn, inquire about me and what I do, and I'm always happy to make the attempt."I write, and I'm flying to _____ to lecture about one of my books." "Oh really. What kind of books do you write?" This is when I agonize as how best to respond. I try to be as truthful as possible but people can be superstitious and fearful and not everyone will be enriched by exposure to things that disturb them for one reason or another. Why spoil the few hours we have together? Perhaps it is best to change the subject to pleasant things in life we have in common, like movies, and food, or bragging about how well our children and grandchildren are doing. But I almost always take the bait and end up saying something like, "My newest book is about Magick, tarot cards, and the Hebrew Qabalah."

Dead silence. Blank stare. Or, if I'm lucky, *they* change the subject. If I'm *not* lucky they become actually interested and ask, "Magick? Oh! That sounds interesting. Tell me about magick."

It's a well-known fact of esoteric life that there is no such thing as "Magick 101." Even on a fourteen-hour flight to Beijing it is impossible to properly introduce anyone to Magick. But do I ever learn? No.

After explaining that Magick with a "k" is not pulling a rabbit out of a hat or sawing a woman in two, I try to start at the beginning. "Well do you know about the Sumerians?" I might ask. "They were big before the

Egyptians . . . very strange folks, the Sumerians . . . well, they saw everything in life as a hierarchy of natural forces that they identified (metaphorically) as gods, angels, and demons which they attempted to influence and control. They organized this unseen population in anal-retentive detail according to their understanding of elements, planetary spheres, zodiac signs . . . *bla bla bla.* . . .

You've probably heard of the *Egyptian Book of the Dead?* Right! Well *that* was really cool—sort of a state-of-the-art how-to manual that taught how to actually manipulate frequencies of consciousness as we pass through phases of the death coma . . . *bla bla bla.* . . .

The Greeks figured out that existence, time, space and *everything*, are merely aspects of consciousness . . . *bla bla bla.* . . .

Then a bunch of very smart Jewish guys (called Qabalists) loved what the Greeks were doing with numbers and started playing with consciousness in breathtakingly elegant mathematical terms, and organized infinite amounts of abstract information in perpetually replicating fractals of alpha-numeric patterns that when observed would explain everything (*if we just look hard enough at anything.*) . . . *bla bla bla.* . . .

Christian mystics and ecstatic Islamic saints eventually observed that Love (yes, *Love*) is the true nature of reality, and that Love can be focused as an actual, objective, living force as tangible as gravity. And if we get really good at falling in Love we can trigger within ourselves the big cosmic awakening that Christ and all the saints and Holy people have been talking about for thousands of years . . . *bla bla bla.* . . .

Abra-melin the Mage tried to explain it all by revealing that each of us is possessed with a personal god that he called the Holy Guardian Angel which is really the embodiment of the Love force ... *bla bla bla.* ...

Alchemy ... bla bla bla. ...

Have you heard of the Rosicrucians? Well, they were like alchemists but with an agenda! Nobody knows who they really were ... or even if they ever really existed, but I guess it doesn't matter because they wrapped up some of the coolest ideas of Greek hermeticism along with mystic Christianity and by doing so accidentally triggered the Protestant Reformation ... *bla bla bla.* ...

Freemasonry loved all this qabalistic, alchemical and hermetic stuff because it could be rationally and intellectually approached, so they tried to wake up everybody by asking smart folks to look at all everything in life, including politics, from logical and scientific point of view. Soon everyone was realizing how silly and superstitious is was for people to believe that kings and queens were any better than they were, and that it was stupid that nations kept having wars with each other. So, the Freemasons institutionalized everything under the banner of the "Universal Brotherhood of Man." Well, that triggered the "Enlightenment" and inadvertently started the French and American Revolutions ... *bla bla bla.* ...

Oh my God! did I mention the Knights Templar? Now *there's* a story! ... *bla bla bla.* ...

Elphas Levi said all this stuff should rightly be called "Magic!" Oh! and, by the way tarot cards are the flash cards of Qabalah and Alchemy and are connected with the Greeks and the Jews and the Knights Templar and the Rosicrucians and the Masons ... *bla bla bla.* ...

MacGregor Mathers ... *bla bla bla.* ...

Golden Dawn ... *bla bla bla.* ...

Aleister Crowley—they called him a Satanist but if he was a Satanist he was a good kind of Satanist!

I hope you're following this. Oh look! We're landing!

Magick is an art form, and would-be magicians (like all would-be artists) either initially resonate to the styles and forms of the art or they don't. You are either touched and fascinated by Magick's mysteries or you're not. If you *are* so touched, then it doesn't matter what end of the Magick pool you dive into, it's going to be the deep end. No matter where or how you start your journey, *that* is where you begin.

Today we are blessed (and cursed) with the internet, and with the opportunity to have at our fingertips the collective knowledge of the ages. Technical and philosophical questions that only a few short years ago could have only been answered by visiting a library and combing stacks of books (many needing to be translated), or by enrolling in post-graduate university courses, can now be researched and answered in seconds while sitting in your underwear at home.

It's true. We have the "Knowledge of the Ages" at our fingertips. But unless we can digest and apply that knowledge for our own enlightenment we have not earned the "Wisdom of the Ages." Wisdom is what occult studies are about, and Wisdom doesn't come from reading. Wisdom comes only as the by-product of self-realization and self-transformation, and *that's* what magick is about.

The occult revival of the late nineteenth century was a watershed for all who resonate with the art of magick. Ignited in part in 1875 by the foundation of the *Theosophical Society* and the works of Helena Petrovna Blavatsky and others, the English-speaking world was introduced to the sublime subtleties of Buddhism, Hinduism, and yoga. Health movements and metaphysical new-thought mutations of Christianity gave progressive adherents permission to think outside the orthodox box. German, French, Russian, and English "Rosicrucian" societies scoured ancient libraries for medieval grimoires, alchemical and qabalistic texts, and fragments of magical and Hermetic manuscripts written in Greek, and Hebrew and Latin.

In 1888, *The Hermetic Order of the Golden Dawn* was formed, and (primarily through the efforts of its visionary chief adept, Samuel MacGregor Mathers), ingeniously churned the cream of two-thousand years of esoteric systems and practices, into rich magick butter—a Masonic-style, degree-structured initiatory society—breathtakingly Egyptian in motif, and patently qabalistic in structure. For a few short years, the Golden Dawn served as a "one-stop-shopping center" of magick, and (for English-speaking aspirants) it was the only game in town.

Unfortunately, it was a secret game. The players were bound by terrifying oaths never to reveal the details of the instruction, practices, ceremonies, or the names of other members. Predictably, human frailties, infighting and, schism brought an awkward and early end to the Golden Dawn in the first years of the twentieth-century. Various "continuations" of the original organization including the *Stella Matutina* (a very active Golden Dawn hybrid that served as young Israel Regardie's "Golden Dawn.") continued to operate sporadically with varying degrees of success. But the secret rituals and knowledge lectures were soon published, and the golden-years of the Golden Dawn would never return to their former glories.

By 1932, when young Israel Regardie penned *The Tree of Life: a Study in Magic,* the occult world had clearly entered the post-Golden Dawn age. The pioneer generation had (with few notable exceptions) disappeared completely or retrenched. Those brave young souls who were about to become the next wave of magicians were (like the curious person sitting next to me on the airplane) not armed with adequate background information necessary for them to make an informed decision about magick. Regardie saw the need for a fundamental, yet comprehensive summary of the world of practical magick as it was understood practiced in the twentieth century, and he took it upon himself to create it. I, for one, am glad he did, because in 1972 when I first read *The Tree of Life,* I was a naïve dilettante, poorly-armed with bits and pieces of tantalizing magical lore and not having a clue as to what the big picture was.

I had never heard of Regardie, and I bought the book simply because I was looking for some information about the diagram called the "Tree of Life" to supplement my preliminary dabbles with hermetic qabalah. Instead I found myself face-to-face with a mini liberal arts education in the histories, theories, and practices of 2,000 years of magical systems and techniques (complete with rare translations and key excerpts from classic documents).

The reader may be a bit put off (as I was) by Regardie's writing style and what appears to be his transparent attempts at sounding overly mature, occult and recondite. Sometimes it just sounds like he's trying to impress us with his brilliant vocabulary. My suspicions were confirmed that this was his intention: At our first meeting in 1976 I happened to mention how hard it was for me to wade through parts of *The Tree of Life*. He laughed and rolled his eyes and confessed,

"Oh, dear God! I was a boy! And wished to prove I was every bit as loquacious as Old Crow."[3]

Overly loquacious or not, *The Tree of Life* stands as a founding document of modern magick that will continue to open the door to Magick for generations to follow.

---

3 i.e. Aleister Crowley.

The Legend of Aleister Crowley

A Study of the Facts

FOREWORD FOR THE 2016 EDITION[1]

*Look! It doesn't matter if Crowley was a Satanist,
he was a good kind of Satanist, and you'll just love
him! Trust me.*

—ROBERT (MAD BOB) PATTON

You've probably heard *things* about Aleister Crowley
(1875–1947). Perhaps you've heard monstrous things—
hideous things—terrifying things—disgusting and
ghastly things. On the other hand, you might have heard
wonderful things—funny things—astonishing things—
inspiring things—even supernatural and sacred things?
Anyone who thinks they know something about Crowley will most likely voice a very strong opinion either
unfavorable or favorable.

Detractors are quick to vilify him as the Devil
himself—insane, perverse, and evil; while his admir-
ers lionize him as a genius; an enlightened holy man; a
saint; a Buddha; *Prophet of a New Aeon.* It's been nearly
seventy years since Edward Alexander (Aleister) Crowley

---

1 Written for P.R. Stephensen and Israel Regardie, *The Legend of Aleister Crowley:
   A Study of the Facts,* Scottsdale, Arizona: New Falcon Publications, 2016.

drew his last breath, and opinions about him remain as passionately polarized as they were in 1930 when *The Legend of Aleister Crowley* was first published.

As you will learn in Dr. Regardie's fine introductory words (penned in 1969), this slim little volume was originally written and compiled by Crowley's friend and publisher, P.R. Stephensen, to serve as a testament *to* (and showcase sampler *of*) Crowley's extraordinary talents and contributions to the world of English literature and philosophy. The book was also an undisguised attempt to mount a rational defense of Crowley's character and reputation that had been mercilessly and irrationally attacked by the press since the turn of the century. Stephensen's efforts to redeem Crowley, however, would not be immediately or universally successful. It saddens me to say that today, eighty-five years after its initial publication, the world needs to read this book more than ever.

The Legend of Aleister Crowley was my first *real* introduction to the personality and works of Aleister Crowley. I first read it at a pivotal season in my own life, shortly after our son was born in 1972. To say it was a watershed moment in my life would be a monumental understatement. I would go on to spend the better part of the next forty years of my life studying Crowley; digesting his writings; meeting and learning from people who had known him when he was alive; practicing his magical and meditation techniques, and attempting to live the philosophy of life he so passionately espoused. However, my first few stumbling encounters with the works of the man who called himself the *Beast 666* were awkward and comically terrifying.

I was a 24-year old failed yogi and fledgling western mystic poseur working my way through the monographs of the *Rosicrucian Order, AMORC*[2], the *Traditional Martinist Order*[3], and the *Builders of the Adytum*[4]. I fancied myself a bit of a heretic and spiritual rebel, but I certainly wanted nothing to do with anything that smacked of black magick or Satanism[5].

Everything I had read about Aleister Crowley up to that point was bad. My occult dictionary listed him as a black magician who ate human flesh and sacrificed 120 babies one year. My blue-haired Rosicrucian elders told me he was the devil himself. My fellow Martinists cautioned me not to even utter his name. My tarot-loving friends in the BOTA warned me that his teachings were sexually perverse, and that he advocated performing grotesque and unnatural sexual acts on tarot cards. But, for some curious reason, the more my mystical colleagues tried to dissuade me, the more fascinated I became. Who was this guy?

As I have written elsewhere, I bought a deck of his *Thoth Tarot* cards . . . then, hysterically gave them away

2 The Ancient and Mystical Order Rose Crucis (AMORC), headquartered at the time in San Jose, California. Established in 1915 by Harvey Spenser Lewis who claimed the organization was the modern incarnation of the ancient Rose-Croix Order (Rosicrucians) which, in turn, was the continuation of the mystery schools of ancient Egypt.

3 The Traditional Martinist Order (TMO), a mystical order of Christian Mystics who follow one branch of the teachings of French philosopher, Louis-Claude de Saint-Martin. At the time of my involvement TMO was closely aligned with the Rosicrucian Order (AMORC).

4 The Builders of the Adytum (BOTA) is primarily a correspondence school of the Western mystery tradition which traces its roots and traditions to the Hermetic Order of the Golden Dawn and esoteric Freemasonry. Founded by Paul Foster Case in 1922 and based in Los Angeles, California, it was led at the time of my involvement by Case's successor, Ann Davies. BOTA focuses primarily on the Hermetic Qabalah and the qabalistic aspecst of the Tarot.

5 At the time I was an ignorant and superstitious young fool who had no idea that "Black Magick" and "Satanism" (as I fearfully imagined them to be) did not exist in objective reality. Today, while I do not call myself either a black magician or Satanist or even care to use the terms to describe what I believe or practice, I know quite a few perfectly brilliant and intelligent individuals who are quite comfortable identifying themselves as such. Everyone I've met is honest and sincere, and in my opinion, as liberated and possessed of high moral integrity as those who follow less colorful and exotic spiritual paths.

. . . then, took them back after talking with Mad Bob, our family friend (and spiritual mentor) who soundly upbraided me for my display of spiritual cowardice.

"Crowley was cool. He was a genius and a holy man. If you're really serious about mastering magick and the Hermetic arts you're going to have to dig deep into what this guy's about."

"But everyone says he was a Satanist. Was he a Satanist?" I asked Bob.

"*No.* He wasn't a Satanist!" Then he paused. "Well, *Yes.* I guess you could say he was." Then he disagreed with himself once more. "No . . . not really!" Finally he said, "*Look! It doesn't matter if Crowley was a Satanist, he was a good kind of Satanist, and you'll just love him! Trust me.*"[6]

I took Bob at his word, and soon after our curious conversation I had the opportunity to read Crowley's *The Book of Thoth*, the work that was written late in his life to accompany the *Thoth Tarot* cards. I felt like a grammar-school student trying to read post-graduate papers on magick, philosophy, alchemy, qabalah, astrology, and comparative religion. Even though I understood only a fraction of a fraction of what I read, I found Crowley to be brilliant, funny, and someone who had obviously mastered the spiritual arts of which he wrote so passionately. Furthermore it became breathtakingly evident to that Crowley had actually achieved the expanded levels of consciousness his magical practices and meditations are designed to trigger.

Crowley was the real deal, I thought. And if that means he was a Satanist, then he was a *good* kind of Satanist . . . *and I just loved him!*

---

6 Lon Milo DuQuette, *My Life with the Spirits*, York Beach, Maine: Red Wheel/ Weiser, 1999, pp. 69-70.

The Book of Thoth, and the Thoth Tarot cards however, provided precious little information about who Crowley was; what his background was; why he was so admired and hated. I wanted to know more. At the time, books by and about Crowley were very rare if they existed at all. One afternoon in a Laguna Beach bookstore a beautiful black cat named Catalina guided me to an odd little book that would provide me a clearer picture of Crowley the man, the poet, and the philosopher.

"Any books by Aleister Crowley?"[7] I asked the owner. . . .

She looked at me as if I asked her for a book about baby torture, and answered that she didn't think she had any Crowley but pointed to the cat sleeping serenely on the second shelf of the bookcase in the adjacent room. "If I have anything it will be in the shelf behind Catalina . . . that is, if you can get her to move."

Sure enough, peeking just behind the somewhat obese feline was what appeared to be a damaged paperbound edition of *The Legend of Aleister Crowley*. It didn't look at all impressive or scary. In fact it looked rather shoddily produced—the cover almost bare of adornment or color with only a simple graphic of *eye in a triangle* and the words:

---

7   At the time, I was still incorrectly pronouncing Crowley's name "Craw-lee" instead of "Crow-ley" (which rhymes with Holy).

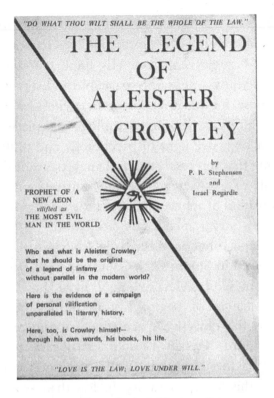

"DO WHAT THOU WILT SHALL BE THE WHOLE OF THE LAW."

THE LEGEND
OF
ALEISTER
CROWLEY

by
P. R. Stephensen
and
Israel Regardie

PROPHET OF A
NEW AEON
vilified as
THE MOST EVIL
MAN IN THE WORLD

Who and what is Aleister Crowley
that he should be the original
of a legend of infamy
without parallel in the modern world?

Here is the evidence of a campaign
of personal vilification
unparalleled in literary history.

Here, too, is Crowley himself—
through his own words, his books, his life.

"LOVE IS THE LAW; LOVE UNDER WILL."

I have to confess the titillating language of the crudely-printed blurbs on the cover intrigued me no end. I stroked Catalina and thanked her, then immediately purchased the book from the shocked proprietor and rushed home to read it.

I was especially impressed with the *Introduction* by Israel Regardie (1907–1985). I recognized the name because I had already read his classic text, *The Tree of Life*[8] as part of my self-guided efforts to learn the qabalah. He had been Crowley's secretary in the late 1920s and lived and with him in France and Germany during an especially colorful period in Crowley's life.

---

8 Israel Regardie, *The Tree of Life: a Study in Magick,* New York: Samuel Weiser, 1972; originally published 1932.

Regardie was just a couple years older than my own father and so in my eyes represented a generational link between Crowley and me. His frank, contemporary writing style was pleasantly palatable and served to lift the verbose, intimidating, larger-than-life Crowley out of the fog of superstitious mythology and place him in the clear objective light of psychology and philosophy. Knowing that this respected and august author thought so highly of Crowley was very reassuring, and the fact he put his seal of approval on this little book profoundly elevated its importance in my estimation.

The signature line of Regardie's *Introduction* revealed that he lived in Studio City, California a little over fifty miles from Costa Mesa where I lived. Suddenly the vaporous fancies of magical history and legend crystalized into the objective space-time coordinates of my own backyard. "Perhaps I could actually meet this guy someday." I thought. (Indeed, the gods soon conspired to make this fantasy a reality. In less than two years I found myself sitting in Regardie's living room in Study City sipping champagne cocktails and discussing magick and Aleister Crowley with my magical neighbor-hero. Regardie and I remained friends until his death in 1985.)

I don't have to remind the reader that 1972 was a long time ago, and the world has changed dramatically in the last thirty-five years. Crowley's reputation, if not totally redeemed, has undergone a fairer, more balanced evaluation in the court of public opinion (at least among the educated and well-informed). Books *by* Crowley and *about* Crowley are abundant and readily available around the world and in many languages. His teachings and occult organizations flourish worldwide, and his contributions to modern art, literature, and philosophy are increasingly acknowledged and recognized.

In 2002 the BBC aired a television documentary, "Great Britons," based on a poll the network conducted to learn who the British people considered the top one hundred "greatest British people in history." There, in 73rd place (nestled comfortably between King Henry V (of Shakespeare fame) and Robert the Bruce (of Mel Gibson's Bravehcart fame), was occultist, ceremonial magician, poet, painter, novelist and mountaineer—*Aleister Crowley.*

I will close these introductory words by heartily encouraging the reader to make the effort if he or she wishes to learn more about Crowley. For me, my labor these last forty years has been well repaid, and my life, my consciousness, and (I dare say . . . my spiritual happiness) has been enriched by the life, the teachings, the magick, and the extraordinary *legend* of Aleister Crowley. I encourage anyone wishing a more thorough and scholarly comment on *The Legend of Aleister Crowley* . . . to also obtain and read Mr. Stephen King's excellent 2007 edition published by Helios Books; and to also avail themselves of Israel Regardie's own biography of Crowley, *The Eye in the Triangle.*[9]

---

9   Israel Regardie, *The Eye of the Triangle,* Las Vegas: New Falcon Publications, 2nd New Falcon edition, 2014; originally published 1932.

The Eye in the Triangle

Introduction to Dr. Israel Regardie's Definitive Work on Aleister Crowley

FOREWORD FOR THE 2017 EDITION[1]

Crowley once said that if a man wanted to begin the study of Magic because he wished to evoke a demon to kill his enemy, that would be all right too. For the student would soon discover the hierarchical structure of the world of magic. That is to say, the demon in question could not be controlled or ordered until the student had made contact with the entity immediately superior. And this entity would only be beseeched to function in terms of his superior—and so on. Very shortly, then, the student would be constrained to invoke, in a direct line, the God or spiritual force ruling over all such operations. In that case, he would have to unite his consciousness with that of the God. By that time, so many transformations in consciousness would have taken place, that the original malefic intent would have disappeared and been replaced by other more worthy and higher aspirations.

—ISRAEL REGARDIE

1   Israel Regardie, *The Eye in the Triangle: Introduction to Dr. Israel Regardie's Definitive Work on Aleister Crowley,* Scottsdale, Arizona: New Falcon Publications, 2017.

I never met Aleister Crowley. He died seven months and eleven days before I was born. No! I *do not* believe I am Aleister Crowley. I have never entertained the fantasy that I *am* or *was* Aleister Crowley. In fact, since earliest childhood I've been haunted by rather clear memory/visions of who I probably *was* in at least one previous life, and I assure you none of these memories have anything to do with Aleister Crowley or, indeed, any person of legendary or notable historical significance.

Over the past forty years, however, because of my dubious reputation as some kind of magical authority, I've been contacted by a fair number individuals who have informed me with straight-faced earnestness they are the living incarnation of Aleister Crowley, the Beast 666, and that I must immediately write a book recognizing them as such. They proffer abundant evidence; qabalistic synchronicities; birthdates, address or telephone numbers, recurring dreams of wild orgies, and shopping receipts totaling $6.66.

When I first met Dr. Francis (Israel) Regardie (1976) we discovered we both had quite a collection of such colorful contacts. We swapped a couple of accounts, then resolved then and there it would be great fun to pool our Crowley incarnation stories and letters in a book that we would title, *Liber Nutz.* We both were half serious about the project and in the years that followed he would occasionally call and send me out to investigate another neighborhood Crowley manifestation. Predictably, the whimsical project never manifested. Regardie died in 1985 and with him *Liber Nutz.*

No matter what you may have read to the contrary on the internet, I was *not* Regardie's "magical apprentice." Nor was I his formal student. I was never "personally initiated" by him into any kind of Golden Dawn, or A∴A∴ or O.T.O.,[2] or anything. I can, however, proudly (and with no small measure of awe and humility) claim him as one of my earliest and most influential magical mentors. He made himself available whenever I had specific questions about magick and Crowley, and he was generous with his time, information and opinions. He was also supportive of our O.T.O. Lodge[3] in Newport Beach, and donated duplicate books from his own substantial library, and other magical trinkets.

Before I met him, however, he was (in my mind at least) an unapproachable god—a mysterious mythological character straight out of the distant legendary past; like Merlin, or John Dee, or Cagliostro, or Woodman and Westcott, Mathers, and *Aleister Crowley*.

In 1972 Constance gave birth to a beautiful baby boy,[4] and the DuQuettes were magically transformed from a young hippy couple to a family. It was also the year I abandoned a drug-energized decade of dangerously successful work as a musician and recording artist, and pretentiously began my Holy Grail quest for respectability and stability. (Forty-five years later I must sadly confess I am still failing spectacularly in this quest.) However, during that youthful transitional period, I did discover something even more precious than the poisonous anesthetizia of American middle-class predictability. I found *Magick*, and the works of Edward Alexander (Aleister) Crowley.

---

2   We *were* both members of the Masonic youth organization, the Order of DeMolay, and upon discovery of this fact both stood up, and exchanged the Sign, Grip, and Secret Word of a DeMolay initiate.
3   Heru-ra-ha Lodge, Ordo Templi Orientis, chartered Jan. 7th 1978 by Hymenaeus Alpha, 777 (Grady L. McMurtry). H.R.H Lodge is the first local O.T.O. Lodge chartered under the auspices of the Grand Lodge of the United States, and remains the oldest continuously operating O.T.O. body in the world.
4   Our son, Jean-Paul Lafayette DuQuette . . . still our heart's delight.

As any magician will tell you, magick isn't *anything* like most people think it is. In fact, magick isn't anything like *anyone* thinks it is. Magick stops being magick when someone can explain it to you; and magick stops being magick when you think you can explain it to others. It's a real paradox, and it's supposed to be a paradox. It's all very *Zen.*

Still, for some of us, we are irresistibly drawn to the art-form of magick (and make no mistake, magick is a most colorful and powerful spiritual *art-form*), not because we believe it is the only path to enlightenment (or even that it is a good one), but because something magical (already bubbling away inside us) tells us it is *our path.*

In 1928, a twenty-year old British-born American art student, Francis Israel Regudy (later Regardie), was snared by this attraction and bravely abandoned his privileged family home in Washington D.C. and set sail for Paris to become a live-in disciple of the notorious Aleister Crowley, the self-proclaimed *World Teacher* and *Prophet of the New Aeon.*

As the reader will soon discover, *The Eye in the Triangle* is Regardie's extended commentary on his years with the Great Beast and the life and works of his infamous former employer. Moreover, the book is an attempt at an insightful, if not completely objective, analysis of the psychological processes that caused *Crowley* to "tick" so peculiarly. At the same time Regardie's observations might also give us some insight as to what might have been making *Regardie* "tick" so peculiarly.

You may find much in *The Eye in the Triangle* that is dated by today's psychologically sophisticated standards. Jung is no longer so new and daring, and as far as sexual matters go there is very little that today unsettles us in the least.

In the mid 1970s when I first read *The Eye in the Triangle* it was the only proper biography of Crowley available. John Symonds' 1951 laughably bad, *The Great Beast*[5] and Crowley's own *Confessions of Aleister Crowley*[6] (wonderful, but hardly complete or objective) were pretty much the only things I could get my hands on. Things are mercifully better for students today, and Dr. Richard Kaczynski's, *Perdurabo—The Life of Aleister Crowley*,[7] will likely remain the most complete, accurate, and objective Crowley biography for many years to come.

As an apologist for Crowley, Regardie must be given high marks for rising above the cruel, small, and nasty injuries Crowley inflicted upon him as a young man in the years following their association. I believe it was not easy for him to do this. I don't believe he did it as some form of *12-Step* forgiveness gesture to make himself feel better in his final years. Rather, I simply believe he came to a place in his life where he could put the entire wonderful and painful experience in prospective; he recognized that the brilliance of Crowley's genius transcended and eclipsed his myriad (and serious) human flaws; he recognized it was his duty to mankind—his duty to the advancement of human thought—to allow the world to see the blazing sun of Crowley's genius and the soul-liberating message he tried to deliver.

Obviously, I am a very big admirer of Crowley and his work (this is due in large part to Dr. Regardie and his various works on the subject of magick.) I sing Crowley's praises a lot. I write books that are extended

---

5 John Symonds, *The Great Beast—The Life of Aleister Crowley*, London: Rider and Company, 1951.

6 Aleister Crowley, The Confessions of Aleister Crowley—an Autohagiography, London: Mandrake Press, 1929.

7 Richard Kaczynski, *Perdurabo—The Life of Aleister Crowley*, Berkeley: North Atlantic Books; revised edition, 2010.

commentaries on Crowley's works. He constantly amazes and inspires me. He is my Holy Prophet. On the other hand, in reading Crowley I will run across something he said or wrote sometime during his seventy-two incredible years that shocks me—that disgusts me—that outrages me. I know for certain that I would *not* have liked Aleister Crowley on a personal level. We would not have gotten on. In that respect, I'm glad he's dead.

But . . . Crowley was a genius.

Have you ever been (un)lucky enough to spend time in close proximity to a real, over-the-top *bona fide* genius for any length of time? an artist? a writer? a filmmaker? a dancer? a mathematician?

I have.

It's hard! It's frustrating. Sometimes it's even dangerous! . . . not because the genius is trying to be a rude, thoughtless and arrogant. To we mortals it may seem like the genius is behaving like an insane jerk. But the genius, more often than not, is completely oblivious (or unconcerned) to the effects he or she has on others. It's because the *art* of the genius is the *soul* of the genius. The body, the mind, the personality, the character, the appetites, the dreams, the hopes, the fears are only servants to their art—and God help anyone or anything that gets in way of the genius and his or her *art*.

Crowley was a genius, and his body of work is a masterpiece—just as real a masterpiece as a Beethoven Symphony, or a painting by da Vinci, or a work by Michelangelo.

It's true, Aleister Crowley had many monstrous shortcomings, but so did Beethoven and da Vinci and Michelangelo. They all were mad as hatters. They still created immortal, consciousness-elevating works.

Through their genius, they manifested truth. And truth is bigger than any fragile and illusionary personality. It took Regardie many years to put behind him the stings of personal injuries he suffered from Crowley's penpoint; but he eventually did; and we are all enriched his act of posthumous magnanimity.

The image of the "Eye in the Triangle" of course has many magical and mystical connotations. It is certainly a profound and appropriate title for Regardie's treatment of the life and works of Aleister Crowley. I believe, however, that it also represented the opening of Regardie's own eye to the spiritual significance of Crowley's contribution to the evolution of human consciousness, and to the importance of his own vital role and responsibility in presenting it to the world.

And now, I don't wish to take more of the reader's time with these introductory words. So, I would like to close with something I wrote over thirty years ago for my own amusement and for the amusement of my friends and colleagues who knew and loved Dr. Francis (Israel) Regardie.

Shortly after Regardie died in 1985, testimonials and memorials poured into the handful of occult and metaphysical-themed publications. Most of these *In Memoriams* had one thing in common; they nearly all spent a great deal of the article telling the reader how much *Regardie* admired and respected *them!* I was embarrassed and somewhat ashamed of my magical colleagues for their tasteless exploitation of the moment, so I wrote a parody (under a magical *nom de plume*) mocking their self-serving articles. I prevailed upon a sympathetic editor of prominent esoteric magazine of the day who was kind enough to publish it. If you think it sounds ridiculous and absurd . . . . believe me . . . it is not nearly as ridiculous and absurd as some of the "real" *In Memoriams* published after his death,

This silly little parody is my most sincere thank you gift to Regardie; my way of telling him how much I truly loved, respected, and admired him. I know he would be laughing the loudest.

ISRAEL REGARDIE
HIS FAVORITE STUDENT REMEMBERS
By Frater Stonehenge Equinox
(As told to Lon Milo DuQuette)

It wasn't long after Israel Regardie met me that his health began to fail. Even though we met in person only twice I still managed to have a profound effect upon his life. They say you never have a second chance to make a good first impression, and, if I say so myself, Regardie's first impression of *me* was a lasting one.

At the time, I did not know his address, so I staked out his Post Office box in Studio City. After three days, he finally arrived to pick up his mail. He almost missed his chance to meet me for, alas, I had fallen asleep on the sidewalk near the newspaper racks in front of the building. Destiny, however, could not be thwarted and the gods guided his tiny footsteps to tread upon my left hand and forearm.

Luckily, he was not hurt badly in the fall, and as I helped him gather his mail from the gutter I seized the opportunity to introduce myself.

"Equinox is my name, Stonehenge Equinox. You're the reason I'm into magick."

He responded with an astounding display of mental telepathy.

"I don't suppose you're insured?" he asked (not concealing the fact that he already knew the answer).

I followed him to his car where I displayed my tattoos and treated him to an impromptu performance of my original *Diagonal Pillar Ritual*. He feigned disinterest, but I could tell he was favorably impressed. Great magicians don't need words to communicate with each other, and so I was not surprised to see him speed off in his car without uttering a sound (although he did gesture).

Our next meeting was more mystical and intimate. As providence ordained, I found his phone number scrawled on the restroom wall at the *Bodhi Tree Bookstore* in West Hollywood and immediately gave him a call. Playfully disguising my voice, I told him I had thrown my back out and made an appointment for a chiropractic adjustment.

There's no question that the man was omniscient, but he seemed genuinely surprised to see me when I and my (then) girlfriend, Diana Ishtar Sophia Morgana, appeared at his door.

The dear man asked if I had come for the spinal adjustment, and voiced his delight that I had brought someone to help me home. What a saint! And you know, he was right. After his treatment, I was unable to walk for three weeks!

Thus began a five-year odyssey of intense spiritual correspondence. Every Friday I mailed him my magical record, dream diary, semen sigils, and excerpts from my (still) unfinished novel, *Sex Wizards of Phlegm*. Each week, like clockwork, my letters and packages were returned to me seemingly unopened and unedited.

However, to a trained clairvoyant such as myself, adept in traveling in the spirit vision, these "silent messages" were a treasure-chest of deeply personal magical instruction and encouragement. Each page dripped with his energy and all were alive with psychically transmitted practical advice, initiatory ordeals, and occult secrets. It was in this manner that he consecrated me "Psychopomp of North Hollywood."

Then, shortly before his death, he chose to abandon our astral correspondence and communicate to me on the material plane by actually writing me a letter. It was in this last letter that he poignantly revealed his deep personal affection for me by beginning his message by addressing me as "Dear. . . ."

It was also in this letter that he revealed a mystic precognition of his own impending death.

After advising me on matters of mental health, personal hygiene and the proper use of the English language, he closed with these chillingly prophetic words . . .

"It will not be necessary for you to *ever* contact me again!

How to Make and Use Talismans

FOREWORD FOR THE UNPUBLISHED SECOND EDITION[1]

Magick is the Science and Art of causing change to occur in conformity with Will.

—ALEISTER CROWLEY

I am a magician. For nearly 30[2] years I have, by means both traditional and forbidden, endeavored to cause changes to occur in my life in conformity to what I have perceived to be my Will. I say "perceived" to be my Will, because it is not until one has developed a significant level of illumination that one can with any degree of certainty know what one's Will really is.

Please don't assume that just because I have practiced magick for such a long time that I possess an unclouded vision of my true Will or that I consider myself an illuminated master. I do not. What I do possess, however, is a great deal of magical experience, and experience is the potential breeding-ground of wisdom. Naturally, that potentiality disintegrates if I can't remember these experiences so that I might apply their lessons to my magical life. For this reason, it is vitally important that a magician keep a record of his or her exploits.

---

1 Written for an unpublished second edition of Israel Regardie, *How to Make and Use Talismans*. New York: Samuel Weiser, Inc., 1972.

2 This written in 2001.

For me, reviewing old magical diaries is never a pleasant experience. Every time I open and read one of my ancient journals I am paralyzed by a combination of nauseating embarrassment and wonder. I grit my teeth and squirm as I relive the thoughts and dreams of that shallow, self-centered, naive, ego-blinded young fool who gawked back at me from the mirrors of yesterday.

Painful as it has been, reviewing my magical records has afforded me the opportunity to chart the general trajectory and momentum of my spiritual evolution. I have even been able, in several instances, to pinpoint the exact minute my magical efforts have actually caused change to occur in conformity with my Will—times that have dramatically changed my life, and the lives of others. In fact, at this very moment, *you* are reading the words on this page as the result of a magical operation I set in motion twenty-six years ago. As a matter of fact, it was twenty-six years ago today.

In the autumn of 1974 I was enmeshed in what I will politely described as a turning point in my life. I was twenty-six years old, married, with a two-year-old son. I was desperately trying to wean myself from a very unhealthy career as a musician and struggling to bring some semblance of stability and direction to my life. Several years prior to this, to address an intense spiritual hunger, I entered the initiatory world of the Western Mysteries—specifically, the degree work of the *Rosicrucian Order, AMORC* and the *Builders of the Adytum (BOTA)*.

As fascinating as my studies were, they were just that—studies. My life needed changing. I didn't want to just study magick; I wanted to perform magick—but what kind of magick? I had heard some pretty scary things about the evils of magick, so I was desperate to find a safe place to start.

Early in January 1975, in an old and stuffy little occult bookstore in North Long Beach, I purchased *How to Make and Use Talismans* by Israel Regardie. I trusted Regardie, having read several of his classic magical texts. This little book, however, was different. It was actually a how-to book of practical magick. Regardie's sane and straightforward explanation of the fundamentals of talismanic magick instantly dispelled my superstitious doubts. His generous offering of charts, diagrams and illustrations (which I promptly copied and pasted into my magical diary) made it a treasure-trove of easy-to-use information. I couldn't wait to graduate from student to practitioner. After reading it through several times I knew exactly where I needed to begin.

In Chapter Two, Regardie suggests that planetary talismans can be helpful in overcoming unfavorable aspects that might be afflicting one's astrological chart. I knew I had difficult aspects in my natal chart so I contacted my brother, Marc (the astrologer), to see which planet could use a little extra help. "All of them," he coldly informed me. But, because it rules my chart, he suggested I first try to make friends with the Moon.

With Regardie's little book as my guide, I started gathering symbols for a Lunar talisman on January 23. At midnight on the 27th, after anointing it with drops of dew that had formed in the moonlight falling on my 1952 Chrysler, I consecrated it with as much ceremony as I was capable of devising.

My Moon talisman was the most beautiful thing I had ever made. It was a double circle model made of card stock. I extracted the sigils of the Lunar spirit and intelligence from the kamea in the book and carefully drew them in silver paint against a field of deep violet drawing ink on the front and back of one of the circles. On the other circle I painted a sliver image of the elephant god, Ganesha (to whom the Moon is sacred) on one side, and on the other side the appropriate planetary and geomantic symbols. Around one perimeter I wrote in Hebrew the divine and angelic names, and on the reverse side part of the 72 Psalm " . . . *abundance of peace so long as the moon endūreth.* " When it was finished I lovingly slipped it inside a linen bag I had sewn with violet thread. On the flap I embroidered a silver crescent moon.

I was very proud of myself, but I still didn't feel like much of a magician. I did carry it around for a few days and felt tremendously empowered—but empowered to do *what* I didn't know. I wasn't sure what I should do next. The answer came (as so many important answers do) while I was taking a shower. I should make all of the planetary talismans!

For the next four months, with the help of Regardie's *How to Make and Use Talismans* and using my ever-improving artistic and magical skills, I created and consecrated a full set of seven planetary talismans. Each one was more beautiful and worshipful than its predecessor. The order in which I created them was dictated by the severity of the planetary afflictions in my natal chart. I consecrated the Mars talisman on February 12. By then I had taught myself the Supreme Invoking Ritual of the Pentagram and Hexagram which from then on became part of my consecration rituals.

Jupiter was next on February 27, followed by Venus exactly one month later. The Venus talisman evoked the most remarkable reactions. My dreams were filled with vividly erotic encounters such as I had not experienced since adolescence. They continued until April 4 when I consecrated my talisman of Mercury when my dreams turned anxious and confusing. (Oh well!)

I started the Saturn talisman on May 10th and consecrated it at midnight on the 13th. The next day I started to collect the symbols for my seventh and last planetary talisman. Sol took 10 days to complete. I consecrated it during a lunar eclipse that took place on May 24th. My arsenal of planetary talismans was finally complete.

Throughout this entire talisman-making period and the months that followed, life at the DuQuette house was a litany of chaos, frustration and despair. In an attempt to make money doing something other than singing in saloons, I accepted a house-painting job and we moved to the San Gabriel Valley. As it turned out I would never be paid for my (admittedly inept) labor and we found ourselves stranded in the smoggiest town in California with no job and no money.

July 11th dawned with the prospect of the worst birthday of my life. About 11:15 in the morning I shut myself in my bedroom temple. I lit a candle and put it on my altar top. I half-heartedly performed the banishing rituals of the pentagram and hexagram and sat down and tried to meditate. I couldn't. To cheer myself, I removed my cherished talismans from their bags and lingered on every detail of their splendor. As I turned them in my fingers I whispered the words of power and the names of the gods, angels and spirits inscribed on each one of them. Finally, as if to bring order to my otherwise unordered universe, I placed the Sun in the center of the altar top and surrounded it with the six remaining planets in their proper hexagram positions. They were so beautiful—so perfect.

For a moment I didn't know how to feel. I was alternately depressed and elated—depressed that these talismans were the *only* things perfect in my life, and elated that at least *something* was perfect in my life. I looked at the clock. It was almost noon and time to rejoin my wife and son for birthday cake. They were both giggling in the kitchen. Their laughter made me giggle too, and in a cliché epiphany worthy of a Frank Capra film, I realized that there were *lots* of perfect things in my life.

My melancholy lifted. I credited the talismans for my change of mood. As I gazed at them there on the altar top I realized that they would never be more beautiful or meaningful to me than they were at that moment. In just a few weeks their colors would start to fade, the inks would crack, the edges wear. In a few years I would probably lose some of them, and those that remained would shrivel into crumbling corpses. How could I preserve them forever just like this—at the zenith of their strength—in an environment where their beauty would never be effaced—a place where their power would never diminish? There was only one answer, and it returned to me on the same thought-wave that had carried my question.

These talismans were no good to me sitting on my altar top or tucked away in their sterile little bags. They would have to literally become part of me. No! More than that—I must use their magick to make me *someone else*—someone new. I must reabsorb my precious planetary children and plant them in the womb of my own soul. I must impregnate myself with their magical potency and by doing so beget upon myself a *new* self.

One by one I joyously plunged the seven talismans into the magick fire of the altar candle, and inhaled their light and heat as the frail husks of paper and ink were reduced to a clean white ash.

It was noon, July 11, 1975—the first moment of my life as a magician.

PART TWO

CLASSICS OF MAGICK

~~~~~~~~~~

Students of the Western magical traditions often disagree on any number of the finer points of the art, and how they should or not be applied in practice. There are those who adore Aleister Crowley for his brilliant wit and audacity, and those who despise him for his morals and lifestyle. There are those who will argue the objective reality of spirits and demons, and those who will argue that even objective reality is subjective. But one thing almost all students of magick (at least those who have been studying for a few years) have in common is our *libraries*.

It doesn't matter if you consider yourself "Left Hand Path" or "Right Hand Path," alchemist or sorcerer, Christian mystic, or Thelemic magician, it is highly likely you have *The Book of Abramelin* (or the *Sacred Magic of Abramelin the Mage*), and *Light on the Path*, and *The Cloud Upon the Sanctuary*, and the works of Jon Dee, and Georg von Welling, and of course, Donald Michael Kraig's *Modern Magick*.

Over the years it has been my honor and privilege to introduce new generations of magicians to these classic texts and take great pleasure to present them to you.

A True and Faithful Relation of What Passed for Many Years Between Dr. John Dee and Some Spirits

INTRODUCTION TO THE 1992 EDITION[1]

On July 20, 1550 the academic community of Paris was ablaze with excitement. The auditorium of Rhemes College was filled to overflowing with the most learned men of Europe. Passionate young students crowded the eaves and pressed hungry ears to the windows to hear an unprecedented lecture on mathematics.

The speaker was an extraordinary young Englishman whose commentaries upon the propositions of Euclid had stunned and delighted the great minds of the University at Louvain and court of Charles V at Brussels. Not yet thirty years old, he was being hailed as the "New Agrippa," the heir to the great Philosopher–Magicians and the first English "Magus."

His name was John Dee and he was destined to become the "ornament of the Age," one of the most influential figures of Renaissance England . . . also one of the most vilified.

---

1 Written for John Dee, *A True and Faithful Relation of What Passed for Many Years Between Dr. John Dee and Some Spirits.* New York: Magickal Childe, 1992 (facsimile of 1659 edition).

To adequately profile the life and accomplishments of John Dee would require a series of tomes the size of the one you are now holding. Yet with very few exceptions, it has only been recently that biographers have begun to scratch the surface and explore the incredible details that have been denied to the public for over three hundred years.

He was mathematician, physician, mechanician, geographer and chemist. He was tutor to royal families both in England and abroad. His private book collection at his home in Mortlake was Elizabethan England's great library. He was engineer, antiquarian, scientist and theologian. No vain dablerk, he was master of these and a score of other arts and sciences. His inventions and contributions profoundly affect his world.

Why then is he not celebrated with the other luminaries of the Elizabethan period? Why has his name fallen through the cracks of the history of Western Civilization?

"Caller of Devils, Arch Conjurer, Necromancer, Invocator of damned Spirits, Sorcerer, Witch, Enchanter, Black Magician" . . . these were occupations also attributed to John Dee. These accusations dogged him throughout his lifetime and defined his reputation after his death.

I will not even attempt to elaborate the details of this unbelievably eventful life. I leave that to two most excellent modern biographies: *Elizabethan Magic*[2] by Robert Turner, and especially Peter French's *John Dee, The World of an Elizabethan Magus.*[3] But a brief sketch at this point I think is in order.

---

2   Robert Turner, *Elizabethan Magic: The Art and the Magus*, London: Element Books, Ltd., 1990. Out of print but available used from numerous sources.
3   Peter French, *John Dee, The World of an Elizabethan Magus*, London: Routledge, reissue edition, 1987.

John Dee was born on July 13, 1527 to Rowland Dee and Johanna Wild. The family (who could trace their ancestry to Roderick the Great, an early Prince of Wales) was not wealthy but could boast what could be called a middle-class income. His father, a gentleman server to Henry VIII, was not without connections at court.

In 1542, his father sent him to Cambridge where young Dee budgeted his time to enable him to routinely study eighteen hours a day. Four years later Henry VIII founded Trinity College and Dee received a fellowship as an under-reader of Greek.

At Trinity, he also delighted in the study of engineering and mechanics and he volunteered to be a member of the stage crew in the production of the play PAX by Aristophanes. Amusingly, this was where his reputation as a Black Magician began. His unique mechanical innovations were responsible for seemingly miraculous stage effects. The illusion of the Scarbeus flying up to heaven with a man on its back provoked rumors of supernatural assistance—and indeed, the equipment constructed by Dee to accomplish this illusion incorporated advanced technology and invention not taught at Cambridge.

In 1547, he took his first trip abroad to consult with the learned men of the day in the Netherlands. A year later he received his Master of Arts from Cambridge and enrolled in Louvain. His reputation throughout Europe was startling. Scholars of many countries traveled to confer with him and invitation from kings and emperors were routinely, but politely, refused.

Back in England, however, his reputation as a sorcerer was enhanced when, in 1555, the administration of Queen Mary had him imprisoned because of a false accusation of *Lawde vayne practices of calculing and conjuring* to enchant the Queen. He soon extricated himself from this fall from grace and when Elizabeth was crowned in 1558 Dee was a frequent and welcome visitor at court. He was even given the honor of casting the horoscope determining the date and hour of the coronation ceremony—ironic, as his astrological practice was part of his problem with Queen Mary.

Elizabeth conferred often with Dee on matters of state, international policies and most importantly England's adventurous explorations at sea. His knowledge of geography, history and science was unequaled and many of the remarkable achievements of the Virgin Queen should be credited to his sage council. She became his patron and protector.

This royal protection would be needed, for as his reputation as a Philosopher-Magus grew, so did rumors and accusations of black magic. The vulgar element saw his odd, eccentric genius as proof he was in league with the devil. His study of Hermeticism (a perfectly natural endeavor for a Renaissance scholar) was viewed by many with suspicion and fear. His house and library at Mortlake were ransacked by a mob of neighbors in 1583 while he was on the continent, and he was slandered in print as "Doctor Dee the great Conjurer" by Protestant extremist John Foxe. Dee succeeded in halting the slander but the damage was done.

Dee obviously felt that the discretion he exhibited at home in England would be unnecessary on the more enlightened continent. For six years between 1583 and 1589 he and skryer Edward Kelley practiced various forms of cabalistic and angelic evocation quite openly.

Upon his return to England (at Elizabeth's request) he continued to be harassed and accused. Elizabeth was too distracted with court intrigues to offer much support.

Dee's last years were unhappy. The plague claimed his third wife, Jane Fromand, who mothered all eight of his children. His own health failing, he was pressured by plots of his fellows to give up his position as Warden of Manchester College. He returned to Mortlake with his daughter Katherine who was to be his nurse in the last years.

In December of 1608 after King James I ignored Dee's attempt to clear his name by being tried as a conjurer, Dee died peacefully at Mortlake.

Meric Casubon did not intend to immortalize Dr. John Dee when he published portion of Dee's magician diaries in 1659. Quite the contrary, it is clear that he wished to diminish Dee's considerable reputation by perpetuating a portrait of a gullible and spiritually naïve academician whose unwholesome obsession with dreams of communicating with angels led to his social and financial ruin.

Titillating the reader with warnings that the material, "... might be deemed and termed A Work of Darkness" Casaubon spent the time and considerable expense to vilify the memory of a man considered by many of his contemporaries to be the greatest mathematician and philosopher of his Age, can be discovered in the complex and dangerous intrigues surrounding the social/political/religious upheaval of the Puritan Revolution.

Throughout the Civil War and Commonwealth Period (1642-1660) Casaubon remained a loyal and vocal supporter of the Anglican Church. As a recognized and respected classical scholar he was stunned when in 1644, by order of the government, his position at Canterbury and accompanying salary were suspended.

Disenfranchised, he sought to avenge himself upon the Puritan government by attacking one of the fundamental tenants of the faith; namely, the belief that individuals, independent of the offices and inspiration of the Church, could receive spiritual guidance directly from divine sources.

If Casaubon could demonstrate that even the great Dr. Dee was victim of diabolic deception, perhaps the spiritual *cause célèbre* of Calvin and Cromwell might also be no less a product of Satanic delusion. As he would hang if he publicly state the latter, he chose to attempt to prove the former.

The government of the Commonwealth was indeed upset over the publication a *A True & Faithful Relation of What Passed for many Yeers between Dr. John Dee . . . and Some Spirits* (as Casaubon titled the work). However, so many copies were initially printed and distributed that all official attempts to suppress it failed.

In the minds of the public, the rumors of Dee's involvement in "Black Magic" were true—confirmed by his own words, in his own diaries. Casaubon had succeeded in sacrificing the reputation of Renaissance England's greatest Philosopher-Magus upon the altar of vulgar expediency.

Nevertheless, we owe Meric Casaubon a profound debt of gratitude; for no matter how unworthy his motives, his work has served as an ark—a time capsule which has preserved one of the most remarkable magical records of all time.

THE METHOD OF SCIENCE, THE AIM OF RELIGION

To the modern student of magic, *A True and Faithful Relation* . . . is a treasure without equal. We experience almost voyeuristic self-consciousness as the intimate nature of the record unfolds. We become eaves-droppers on the details of the most remarkable magical event ever recorded.

To Dee, Magick was Science. He took excellent notes; recording each experience with the precision of modern scientific notation. He did not wish to talk with Angels so he could bewitch his neighbor's cow or seduce the girl next door. He sincerely desired more information about the laws of nature and the underlying principles of Creation.

Like Henry Cornelius Agrippa and Giordano Bruno, Dee was conscious of the fact that he was perhaps the most learned man of his day. Everything that was known to Man was known to him. He was the world's foremost author-ity on a score of subjects from geography to mechanics. Where does a man who knows more than another person on earth turn when *he* still has questions. The answer was God, or more accurately, God's messengers to Man, The Angels who throughout biblical literature appeared to pious men to teach the knowledge that was hidden from mortals. The Patriarch Enoch was once such man who found favor in the presence of God—hence Dee used the word "Enochian" to describe his efforts.

From 1582 to 1589 Dee and his "skryer," Edward Kelly, plunged almost daily into the black obsidian mirror that was their doorway to the "Angelic" world. Despite his somewhat dubious reputation, Kelly was a gifted clairvoyant. It was obvious from the earliest sessions that something extraordinary was taking place. Both men seemed genuinely surprised by the success of the initial contacts, the awkwardness of these early session is touchingly amusing.

Questions concerning world politics and matters of State dominated these first encounters but as the sessions continued it became clear that the Angels had an agenda of their own.

Dee and Kelly were informed that the Angelic world could be more easily accessed and communications more efficiently facilitated if the magician actually spoke the language of the Angels. The Communicating Angels then proceeded, in the most complex and extraordinary manner, to teach them the angelic language. This event is without parallel in magical history. Israel Regardie in his massive work, *The Complete Golden Dawn System of Magic*[4] writes:

> The Enochian Language is not just a haphazard combination and compilation of divine and angelic names drawn from the [Enochian] tablets. Apparently, it is a true language with a grammar and syntax of its own. Only a superficial study of the invocations suffice to indicate this to be a fact. The invocations are not strings of words and barbarous names, but are sentences which can be translated in a meaningful way and not merely transliterated.

---

4   Israel Regardie, ed., *The Complete Golden Dawn System of Magic,* Las Vegas: New Falcon Publications, 1985; 2nd edition 2008.

Eighteen invocations, or "Calls," written in the Angelic language, comprise a system whereby the magician can access the unseen elemental universe underlying the phenomenal world. A nineteenth Call is used to penetrate the spiritual world known in the system as the Thirty Aethyrs. These correspond roughly to the ascending planes of consciousness of the Qabalistic universe and explored by the magician in the same manner as "path workings.

It is ironic that Dee and Kelly did not utilize much of the technical information dictated to them. They seemed to be almost entirely absorbed in the process of obtaining the data.

It would be over three hundred years before the material Dee and Kelly labored so hard to obtain would be organized into a magical system by Golden Dawn genius S. L. MacGregor Mathers who recognized the intrinsic value of the surviving diary material. The records found in *A True and Faithful Relation* . . . supplied the bulk of this information.

The two major branches of modern practical Enochian Magic (Elemental and Aethyrical) were grafted by Mathers to the Adeptus Minor curriculum of the Golden Dawn. In 1898, Aleister Crowley joined the Golden Dawn and in 1900 attained the Grade of Adeptus Minor. The passion of his exploration of the Enochian system far exceeded the efforts of his predecessors and in 1909, while walking across the North African Sahara, he completed his systematic explorations of the thirty worlds of the Aethyrs and chronicled them in his masterpiece, *The Vision and the Voice.* Hermetic scholars have seriously compared this document to the visionary works of William Blake and the prophetic writings of Ezekiel and Saint John the Divine.

Interest in Enochian Magick has mushroomed extraordinarily in the last ten years[5] and books on the subject command a respectable amount of shelf space in occult bookstores worldwide. Some of the material is excellent, offering the serious student the opportunity of experiencing something unique—a magical system that really works. Sadly, many other works are of less value and, in my opinion, do a disservice to the seeker. Especially disturbing are the presumptuous attempts of some authors to "guide" the vision of readers, intimating that the operations are failures if they do not match those the author suggests should be expected. Recently attempts have been made to standardize the methodology of the operating procedures and create a form of Modern Enochian Orthodoxy which is absurd.

Ironically, the one work that very few student have ever had access to is the one work they would find most interesting and helpful. It is the first Enochian book anyone should read, and until now, it was almost impossible to find.

We own a great debt of gratitude to Herman Slater[6] for making this treasure available to the public. The enduring quality of this edition of *A True and Faithful Relation* . . . will ensure that his remarkable work will survive for centuries to come.

---

5   This passage was written in 1990.
6   1936–1992.

Opus Mago-Cabalisticum Et Theosophicum

In Which The Origin, Nature, Characteristics, And Use Of Salt, Sulfur and Mercury are Described in Three Parts Together with Much Wonderful Mathematical . . .

FOREWORD FOR THE 2006 EDITION[1]

I've studied now Philosophy

And Jurisprudence, Medicine,

And even, alas! Theology

All through and through with ardour keen!

Here now I stand, poor fool, and see

I'm just as wise as formerly.[2]

---

1   Written for Georg Von Welling, *Opus Mago-Cabalisticum Et Theosophicum*. Newburyport, Massachusetts: Weiser Books, 2006.
2   Johann Wolfgang Goethe, *Faust*, trans. by George Madison Priest, New York: Alfred A. Knopf, 1941.

In Act I of Goethe's *Faust*, the melancholic hero broods alone in his chamber and reflects upon the vainness of earthly knowledge and education. He opens a book of magic and gazes in almost sensual wonder upon the lines and symbols on a diagram of the Macrocosm. Upon waves of ecstasy he gives voice to the passion that since the dawn of consciousness has consumed the student of the mysteries.

What rapture, ah! at once is flowing
Through all my senses at the sight of this!
I feel a youthful life, its holy bliss,
Through nerve and vein run on, new-glowing.
Was it a god who wrote these signs that still
My inner tumult and that fill
My wretched heart with ecstasy?
Unveiling with mysterious potency
The powers of Nature round about me here?

Am I a god? All grows so clear to me!
In these pure lineaments I see
Creative Nature's self before my soul appear.
Now first I understand what he, the sage, has said:
"The world of spirits is not shut away;
Thy sense is closed, thy heart is dead!
Up, Student! bathe without dismay
Thy earthly breast in morning-red!"[3]

---

3 Ibid.

The archetype for the book that fired Goethe's imagination, and in the play initiated Faust's memorable career as magus, was in all likelihood a real book—a book of forbidden knowledge that evoked every mystical cliché of the dramatic imagination; a massive and heavily illuminated work of alchemy, astrology, theology, magic, and cabbala which in 1719[4] dropped like a living culture into the fertile medium of western syncretic thought; a book that for the remainder of the 18th century would revolutionize the Rosicrucian, Masonic, and Hermetic movements throughout Europe; a book with which Goethe, and the brightest stars in the firmament of European esotericism were intimately familiar—Georg von Welling's[5] *Opus Mago-cabbalisticum et Theosophicum*.

For the modern student of the western mystery traditions, especially those whose studies and practices spring from the teachings and ceremonies propagated by the Hermetic Order of the Golden Dawn, it would be difficult to overestimate the importance of von Welling's work. It served as the primary instructional text of the *Gold- und Rosenkreuzer* (Golden Rosicrucians), a highly prestigious Hermetic order founded in 1777, whose forms, doctrines, and teachings would infect and energize the worlds of mystic Christianity and esoteric Freemasonry. Indeed, the first degree lecture of the *Gold- und Rosenkreuzer* was lifted almost word for word from the fourth section of Vol. I of von Welling's *Opus*.

A hundred years later the nine-degree initiatory structure of the Golden Rosicrucians would provide

---

4 Von Welling penned the author's foreword to a complete edition on January 4, 1721.

5 Von Welling also wrote under the pseudonym, Gregorius Anglus Sallwigt.

the founding fathers of *Societas Rosicruciana in Anglia* (Rosicrucian Society in England) the archetype for their organization. SRIA's offspring, the Hermetic Order of the Golden Dawn, in turn, would give birth to the magical, hermetic, and New Age movements of the 20th and 21st centuries.

In fact, it does not seem to me too far fetched to suggest that this German Golden Rosicrucian/British SRIA pollination may well have provided the historic basis for the fanciful (and likely unhistorical) legend which suggests the Golden Dawn's authority was derived from a certain German adept whose "colleagues" after her death withdrew their direct support of the Order. But this is a matter best left to the historians of this colorful period.

It's fair for the readers of this new edition to ask, "If *Opus Mago-cabalisticum et Theosophicum* is such an important and historic document, why haven't I heard of it?" The answer is almost unbelievably simple. Significant as the work is, it has until now never been translated into English. For nearly 300 years its mysteries and treasures have been reserved exclusively for those with an eloquent and profound mastery of the German language.

While there is a measure of truth to the statement that a translation of any piece of written material is inferior to the original, the gods have smiled with particular warmth upon this project by alchemically uniting (like *Salt, Sulfur, and Mercury*) the elements of vision and support, in the person of Patricia Baker; the brilliance of the translator, Joseph McVeigh, professor of German Studies at Smith College; and the polished astuteness of Weiser Books, arguably the most venerable English-language publisher of esoteric material in the world.

The result is an historic and invaluable contribution to the universe of esoteric literature.

That being said, it will become almost immediately apparent to even the most knowledgeable and sophisticated reader that von Welling's work is not easy reading. Indeed, much of it, especially those sections concerning Salt, Sulfur, and Mercury, seem to consist primarily of lengthy and redundant ramblings filled with superstitious and comically inaccurate observations of nature and the most *un*scientific of *scientific* conclusions. I confess, before I finished reading the first chapters of Volume One I was having serious doubts as to the relevance of this book, and stopped to ask myself how much more I wanted to learn about salt!

Eventually, as I wearily neared the beginning of Chapter IV of Volume One, I found myself slowing down and synchronizing more comfortably with the unhurried, almost hypnotic pace of von Welling's writing. His avuncular wit began to peek though as I paused to savor how he was saying things. As my blood pressure lowered and my patience rose I found myself surrendering to the images and characters of an archaic and divinely naïve alternate universe—the irrational fairytale reality of the alchemist.

Then, and only then was I in the space where von Welling himself could speak directly to my earlier frustrations:

> However, we must ask for the reader's understanding, that we did not present this material prior to the previous three chapters, as might have been appropriate, for this was not possible according to the mago-cabbalistic approach

to writing. The reader is certainly aware of the manner in which the Holy Spirit "writes," and in which it guided Moses by its most holy power, as he was describing the beginning of creation (which reached its endpoint in the creation of man). However, there is also the mago-cabbalistic style which typically begins with the characteristics or designations of things. We could not proceed in any other manner, than we did, and thus had to follow this style, because the beings concentrated within man represent the characteristics of their own essences, just as the human creature represents the composite character of all of them together.[6]

I cannot, nor do I, expect anyone else to squeeze the comparable blood of illumination from the same turnip of text. What should be universally obvious, however, is the message von Welling seems to be sending to those who have ears to hear—the message that this book is written in a peculiar manner that only those who have already undergone a certain modification to their consciousness will be able to appreciate. Recall the words of Faust:

The world of spirits is not shut away;
Thy sense is closed, thy heart is dead!

By carefully crafting his introductory material von Welling administers an almost psychedelic dose of words

---

6   MS page 136.

and images that opens our *senses* and resurrects our *hearts*—readjusts and redefines our inner vocabulary so that we are all, as it were, on the same page as to the *characteristics or designations of things* he is discussing.

I wish I could say that this modification of consciousness is enough to immediately make the *Opus* easy to comprehend, but unfortunately I cannot. There is yet another layer of cerement that swaths the body of the text that must be unwrapped by the diligent student. It must be remembered that at the time the book was written and published its subject matter touched on themes and theories that if spoken about in plain language would most certainly attract the condemnation and persecution of the church and established academic institutions. The consequences of such negative attention, even in the first half of the 18th century, could be gruesomely unpleasant.

With so many taboos imposed upon published material and public discussion it is impossible to escape the obvious fact that von Welling employed the complex (and for most of the world, incomprehensible) language of alchemy, astrology, magic, and even Holy Scripture to simultaneously conceal his ideas from the profane, while revealing them to the initiated. These, in my opinion, include mystical secrets of the human body and (even more dangerous) the powers and potentialities of human sexuality. After all, what powers do humans possess that are more God-like than those surrounding the conception and birth of another human being—the creation of a perfect vessel for an incarnating soul? This is surely a subject any alchemist worth his *salt* would find eminently suitable for research and experimentation.

While I certainly do not question the sincerity of von Welling's devotion to the Christian faith, it appears in many instances he invokes Deity and quotes scripture not so much as a demonstration of piety but for the benefit of heretic hunters who most certainly would be scrutinizing his work. It is a venerable and effective technique of the cabbalist to camouflage esoteric discourses as scholarly elucidations upon Bible verses. As long as the "Holy Scriptures" were used as the springboard for discussion von Welling remained relatively free to soar to wondrous (perhaps even heretical) heights.

To navigate through this *mago-cabbalistic approach to writing* is a major challenge to the modern reader of ancient alchemical, magical, and cabbalistic texts. One is faced, page after page, with having to hear what is being said in what is *not* being said, and having to ignore what should be ignored in what *is* being said. Still, it is clear von Welling could be audaciously outspoken. In Chapter VIII of Volume Two he doesn't hesitate to rip into his contemporaries in the most uncamouflaged terms:

> We can only wonder at how so many illustrious men could be so wrong in their interpretations of Revelation. On the other hand, their erroneous ways are not surprising when one considers their adamancy, prejudice and arrogance, which prevents them from considering the text correctly.[7]

He sounds like quite a character.

---

7   MS page 394.

I confess most of what I've learned about von Welling has been gleaned from the pages of *Opus Mago-Cabalisticum et Theosophicum*. He was born in 1655 in central Germany near the city of Kassel and until two years before his death in 1727, earned a comfortable living as Director of Building and Mines for the state of Baden-Durlach in southwestern Germany. It is clear that he didn't consider this position just a job. He had a passion for mining and geology and his expertise in these fields is apparent (sometimes to an irritating degree) in his writing. He apparently made no secret of his interest in alchemy as well. Travel literature of the Baden area still proudly points tourists to buildings that once housed his alchemical laboratories.

Von Welling was not an academic snob. As Professor McVeigh's translation artfully demonstrates, he was quite plainspoken, at times even bucolic. Nowhere is his irascible, Mark Twain-like candor more evident than at the beginning of Chapter Five of Volume Three: On Religion According to the Clear and Distinct Meaning of Sacred Scripture and the True Mago-Cabbala, Based on the Same. His words of condemnation aimed at all who would in the name of orthodoxy suppress freedom of thought and exploration ring true today as they did in 1719. I can think of no better way to close this Foreword.

> In the name of God we now move to a topic
> which will surely earn us the censure of ortho-
> dox scholars. Many of these gentlemen believe
> they alone have the right and ability to teach
> and write about theological matters, and that
> priests cannot err in matters of the Law. Thus,
> they will attack anyone who is not a member

of their guild the moment he dares to speak on such topics. They will criticize, fault, judge and condemn in a most unpleasant manner anything he might say that doesn't conform with their ideas. And if they cannot find anything in his statement to criticize or condemn, they are mean enough to simply reject the author's work because he is not a member of their order and was not educated like them in their discipline at the best schools, which they feel gives them the privilege of speaking and writing about theology. However, neither Christ the Lord nor his disciples came from their order of priests and theologians, nor did Christ and His true teachers and disciples attend the top schools of theology. Rather, the disciples studied in the school of Christ and His Holy Spirit. Therefore, no upstanding and enlightened theologian would approve of the insane and downright idolatrous illusions of the orthodox heretic-makers. And so we will not expect a reasonable judgment from them, based on the rules of Christ. Their mocking and faulting will not affect us. And so, let us move on to our principle purpose here.[8]

---

8   MS. page 583.

The Cloud Upon
the Sanctuary

INTRODUCTION TO 2012 EDITION[1]

*The Cloud upon the Sanctuary" has, I believe,
always remained in the memory of a few, and is
destined still to survive, for it carries with it a message of very deep significance to all those who look
beneath the body of religious doctrine for the one
principle of life which energizes the whole organism.*

— *Arthur E. Waite*

Even the most Pollyanna-ish among us will not deny
that there is much unpleasantness in the world around
us; wars and disease, hatred and discord. There seems to
be no limit to the crimes and atrocities our kind is capable and willing to inflict on others of our kind. It's easy
for us to disparage as "evil" the fundamental character of
human nature, and ultimately resign ourselves to lives of
quiet desperation, surviving day-to-day by means of our
moment-to-moment success in choosing the lesser evils.

It is easy to grow cynical and discouraged when
pondering the state of affairs on planet Earth. The
nightly newscasts lay out a dinnertime smorgasbord of
military conflicts, famines, civil unrest, and economic

---

1 Written for Karl von Eckartshausen, trans by Isabel de Steiger, *The Cloud
Upon the Sanctuary,* Weiser Book Collection edition, Newburyport,
Massachusetts: Weiser Books, 2012.

ruin. It is cold comfort to observe that there has never been a season in all of recorded history that has been free of such suffering, injustice, and shameful displays of "man's inhumanity to man." One can argue quite convincingly that civilization, indeed all human enterprise has always been, and forever shall be, driven by the cruel and ignoble motives of greed and avarice of the human heart.

It is also not too much of a jump in logic to assume that all this unpleasantness (which we are helpless to resist or vanquish) is the result of a master plan hatched by villains whose embrace of absolute evil has reached perverted spiritual dimensions.

Everywhere we turn—on the internet, in the newspapers, on television and radio—conspiracy theories and theorists assail us with plots and intrigues hatched by governments and industries (and secret societies that run the governments and industries) who allegedly use information as dis-information to confuse and befuddle us, making us pawns in some monstrous plan for world domination, space alien cuisine, or something transcendently naughty.

Ironically, many of these conspiracy theories and theorists seem to have fallen victim to their own distrust of the obvious, and with the wagging finger of accusatory paranoia have singled out the very organizations and movements most vocally opposed to the evils they fear and despise. Such is danger of trying to out dis-inform the dis-informed.

Thus, the Freemasons, the Rosicrucians, and the Illuminati, societies and movements that were founded upon the most admirable ideals of freedom of thought and the "Brotherhood of Man" are now the "agents of

Satan," or the monolithic Church, or the world bankers, or the Jews, or reptilian space aliens.

At the same time, unless we have allowed ourselves to be completely overwhelmed by the depressing conditions wrought by the world's evils we are forced to acknowledge what appears to be evidence of evolving consciousness—in particular the breathtaking advances in human thought, arts, and sciences—quantum leaps in consciousness that in a few short decades have elevated the conversation from arguments over how many days it took for God to create heaven and earth, to whether or not a particle traveling faster than the speed of light moves backwards in time.

The Theosophic and magical movements of the late 19th century optimistically latched on to the idea that such a master plan does indeed exist—that it is "good"—that it is facilitated by enlightened beings who have transcendently "good" motives, and that humanity advances and evolves spiritually at least partially because of their secret efforts on our behalf. Such is the premise (and the promise) of *The Cloud Upon the Sanctuary*.

The inimitable occultist and writer, Arthur Edward Waite, (who suggested the text to a young and impressionable Aleister Crowley) offers us most thorough and erudite introduction to this edition of the classic work. And it is with particular pleasure that I present it now to you.

Light on the Path

The years between 1875 and 1904 stand as a watershed moment in the history of spiritual movements—it was the moment when the sublime mystical sciences of the East cautiously reached out to touch the awakening consciousness of the materialist West and for a moment it looked as if the meeting heralded the beginning of a beautiful friendship. 1875 saw the births of both the *Theosophical Society* and Aleister Crowley, but it was also starting gun of a migration of 'oriental' ideas and an assortment of "gurus" to the shores of England and America. In 1893, a *World's Parliament of Religions* was held as part of the *World Columbian Exposition* in Chicago. The two-week event was the first major interfaith conclave of spiritual leaders from both the Eastern and Western traditions. Christian Science's Mary Baker Eddy was in attendance, as well as Swami Vivekananda. It could be argued that the ecumenical, new thought, new age, mind-body-spirit movements of the 20th and 21st centuries were born in Chicago in those warm days of September 1893.

It must have been a very exciting time—a season that held the promise of a world united by the common bond of those sublimely simple and universal principles at the heart of all religions and spiritual movements.

---

1   Written for M. C. (Mabel Collins), *Light on the Path*, Weiser Book Collection edition, Newburyport, Massachusetts: Weiser Books, 2012.

Tragically, the insanity of the First World War would all but strangle the child of this enlightened optimism, and the decades that followed would more darkly cloud the vision to all but the most die-hard esotericists.

Eighteen eighty-eight saw the birth of the Hermetic Order of the Golden Dawn in England and in the years that followed a number of documents began to circulate in the magical and Theosophical circles. For all appearance these works had been poised, *waiting in the wings* as it were, for the precisely right moment to be published. The 1897 Mathers translation of *The Sacred Magick of Abramelin the Mage* was one such text that caused a stir among English speaking magicians. It more than any other single work elevated the magical practice of the Middle Ages to the level of the self-transformational disciplines of the East. But for the less flamboyant the tiny book "Light on the Path" written down by M.C. materialized on the scene and was instantly hailed as a modern sacred text *par excellence*.

M.C. was the noted Theosophist and prolific author Mabel Collins (1851 –1927) but she does not take direct credit for its authorship. Indeed, although speculations still abound, it is still not completely clear who might have "dictated" the text or what the circumstances for its creation actually were. The work must stand on its own. It is breathtakingly eloquent in its simplicity, reminiscent of the profound and subtle elegance of the *Tao Te Ching*.

To understand the level of awe in which this little volume was held by contemporary luminaries I can do no better than to refer to the *Introduction* penned by Yogi Ramacharaka (William Walker Atkinson) which would later appear in the Yogi Publications edition. The wisdom of *Light on the Path* is timeless and as fresh and relevant today as it was at the turn of the twentieth century. To both neophyte and adept alike I offer my sincere hope that this little treasure will be a beacon of Light on your Path.

The following treatise, "Light on the Path," is a classic among occultists, and is the best guide known for those who have taken the first step on the Path of Attainment. Its writer has veiled the meaning of the rules in the way always customary to mystics, so that to the one who has no grasp of the Truth these pages will probably appear to be a mass of contradictions and practically devoid of sense. But to the one who a glimpse of the inner life has been given, these pages will be a treasury of the rarest jewels, and each time he opens it he will see new gems.

To many this little book will be the first revelation of that which they have been all their lives blindly seeking. To many it will be the first bit of spiritual bread given to satisfy the hunger of the soul. To many it will be the first cup of water from the spring of life given to quench the thirst which has consumed them. Those for whom this book is intended will recognize its message, and after reading it they will never be the same as before it came to them. As the poet has said: "Where I pass all my children know me," and so will the Children of the Light recognize this book as for them. As for the others, we can only say that they will in time be ready for this great message.

The book is intended to symbolize the successive steps of the neophyte in occultism as he progresses in the lodge work. The rules are practically those which were give to the neophytes in the great lodge of the Brotherhood in ancient Egypt, and which for generations have been taught by guru to chela in India. The peculiarity of the rules herein laid down, is that their inner meaning unfolds as the student progresses on The Path. Some will be able to understand a number of these rules, while the others will see but dimly even the first steps. The student, however, will find that when he has firmly planted his foot on one of these steps, he will find the one just ahead becoming dimly illuminated, so as t give him confidence to take the next step.

Let none be discouraged; the fact that this book attracts you is the message to you that it is intended for you, and will in time unfold its meaning. Read it over and over often, and you will find veil after veil lifted, though veil upon veil still remains between you and the Absolute. It will be noticed by you that the words of the book will remain in your mind, and will become a part of you. You will learn to love this book, and will want it always with you. It will be as music to your soul. To those who know not this book, we would say that it not our work, but was written down by "M. C.," a student of occultism, presumably at the dictation of someone high in authority. Its words and teaching bear witness to the nobility and grandeur of the soul who aspired to it. To us, it is as a guiding star. May it be the same to you. Peace be unto you.

Yogi Ramacharaka

Modern Magick

Twelve Lessons in the High Magickal Arts

FOREWORD FOR THE 2010 EDITION[1]

Magick is not something you do, magick is something you are.

—DONALD MICHAEL KRAIG

I have been privileged in the sixty odd (very) years of this incarnation to count among my friends and colleagues some of the most talented, interesting, and influential personages of the modern occult community. Some, like Israel Regardie, Robert Anton Wilson, Phyllis Seckler, Grady McMurtry, Helen Parsons Smith, Christopher S. Hyatt, and David Wilson (aka S. Jason Black), have (at least for the moment) *shuffled off this mortal coil*; many others, I'm delighted to say, are still here and continue to bless us with their work, wisdom and experience. Occupying a prominent and respected chair among this august circle of adepts is my dear friend, Donald Michael Kraig.[2]

---

1 Written for Donald Michael Kraig, *Modern Magick: Twelve Lessons in the High Magickal Arts,* St. Paul, Minnesota: Llewellyn Publications; revised, expanded ed., 2010.

2 This written in 2010. Sadly, Donald passed away in 2014.

I will no doubt embarrass him with my comments. If so, I must be resolute and remind him that it was *he* who invited *me* to pen the Foreword to this new edition of his classic tome, *Modern Magick*, and that he'll just have to swallow (like the good boy he is) the undiluted medicine of my praise and admiration.

The measure of a magician is not to be weighed against the number of books he or she has written; or the amount of money amassed, or the number of fawning disciples held in tow (although Donald continues to earn a respectable trove of all these things). In the final analysis, the only meaningful credential a magician can present to the world is the *magician*. Has he or she evolved through the agency of magick? Is he or she a wiser, more balanced, more disciplined, more enlightened, more engaged, more self-aware individual? Is the individual a better friend, a better teacher, a better citizen, a better human being because of his or her involvement in this most personal of spiritual art forms? Most importantly, does the magician have the ability to laugh at *magician*?

The world of magical literature is blessed with an abundance of scholars and historians. Magick is, after all, an extremely colorful and fascinating subject. Unfortunately, the field is also cursed with individuals who appear to be exploiting their photographic memories and encyclopedic knowledge of esoterica not as a tool of self mastery and self discovery, but as a vehicle in which to flee themselves and a life of honest self-examination—individuals who make the art of magick their *lives*, rather than applying the art to make their lives *magick*.

If I were to give the novice magician one piece of advice at the beginning of his or her career, it would be, "Study and practice magick, but please! Have a life!" When shopping for instruction, avoid like the plague the pompous, pretentious, paranoid poseur, with little or no sense of humor—steer clear of the "master" who has no interests or vocabulary outside the confines of his or her self-referential magical universe. Most especially, shun those who spend an inordinate amount of time and ink attacking the character and work of rival magicians, authors, teachers and/or anyone else who would dare write and teach on the same subjects.

Donald Michael Kraig is the antithesis of such creatures. It is evident everywhere in his writing. He is profoundly secure in the knowledge of who and what he is. He gives generously of the knowledge and wisdom he has gained from years of study and practice. More importantly he gives generously of himself. In the final analysis, it is all the magician has to give.

PART THREE

QABALAH AND TAROT

~~~~~~~~~~~~~~~~~~~~~~~~~~~~~

Qabalah (or Kabbala or Kabalah or Cabala) is a huge subject with ancient roots and a broad range of traditional, orthodox religious, nonreligious, hermetic, meditative and magical applications. Nineteenth-century magicians could not ignore the obvious qabalistic structure of the Tarot and the ease with which the archetypal images on the cards expressed the esoteric meanings of the letters of the Hebrew Alphabet and other classic qabalistic principles—for the modern magician Tarot and Qabalah are inextricably linked.

Q. B. L.

Being a Qablalistic Treatise on the Nature and Use of the Tree of Life

---

"I, _____ a member of the Body of God, hereby bind myself on behalf of the Whole Universe, even as I am now physically bound unto the cross of suffering, that I will lead a spiritual life, as a devoted servant of the Order; that I will love all things; that I will experience all things and endure all things; that I will continue in the Knowledge and Conversation of my Holy Guardian Angel; that I will work without attachment; that I will work in truth; that I will rely ultimately upon myself; that I shall realize my True Will; that I will interpret every phenomenon as a particular dealing of God with my Soul.

And if I fail therein, may my pyramid be profaned, and the Eye closed to me."

AS I WROTE IN THE PREFACE TO W. H. MÜLLER'S
POLARIA. THE GIFT OF THE WHITE STONE;[2]

---

1 Written for Frater Achad, *Q.B.L.: Being a Qabalistic Treatise on the Nature and Use of the Tree of Life,* Newburyport, Massachusetts: Weiser Books, 2005.
2 From *The Starry Wisdom,* by Lon Milo DuQuette, Preface to *Polaria,* by W. H. Müller, Albuquerque: Brotherhood of Life Publishing, 1996, p. 7.

"The above declaration is known as the 'Oath of the Abyss.' Whosoever utters it with full magical intention invokes a terrible curse upon themselves, for they are either hopelessly deluded and committing an act of supreme spiritual presumption; or they have balanced and perfected all aspects of what most of us consider to be the "self" and are now prepared to take the last irrevocable step toward becoming more than human. In both cases, the world will presume they have gone mad."

On the summer solstice of 1916 Charles Robert John Stansfeld Jones (Frater Achad)[3], an accountant from Vancouver, and A∴ A∴ Neophyte (1° = 10$^{\square}$)[4], formally took the Oath of the Abyss, thereby laying claim (in accordance with the traditions of that august fraternity) to the initiatory title Master of the Temple (8° = 3).

Jones dutifully reported this event in a telegram to Aleister Crowley, his superior in the Order, who nine months earlier in September labored in vain (he thought) to beget a child with his "Scarlet Woman" Jeanne Robert Foster.[5] Crowley was amazed by circumstances of Jones' initiation and the timing of the event. He wrote in his *Confessions* . . .

"Every cause must produce its proper effect; so that, in this case, the son whom I willed to

---

3 (1886—1950). "Achad," Hebrew for "One" and "Unity."

4 The initiatory Grade structure of the A∴ A∴ represents progressively higher states of consciousness and is symbolized as a climb up the ten Sephiroth (emanations) of the Qabalistic diagram known as the Tree of Life. The lowest (1° = 10$^{\square}$) is the lowest (Neophyte). The 1° indicates it is the first degree of the system, and the 10$^{\square}$ indicates that the degree represents the level of consciousness embodied in the 10th Sephira, Malkuth.

5 Jeanne Robert Foster (*neé* Olivier, 1884—1970) her magical motto was Soror Hilarion.

beget came to birth on a plane other than the material ... What I had really done was therefore to beget a Magical Son. So, precisely nine months afterwards, that is, at the summer solstice of 1916, Frater O.I.V. (the Motto of C. Stansfeld Jones as a Probationer) entirely without my knowledge became a Babe of the Abyss."[6]

Jones' remarkable success also represented in Crowley's mind a stunning validation of the A∴A∴ system of magical attainment. The proud "father" gushed ...

"I could only conclude that his success was almost wholly due to the excellence of the system which I had given to the world. In short, it was the justification of my whole life, the unique and supreme reward of my immeasurable toils."[7]

Crowley's confidence in Achad was further bolstered by a string of discoveries Jones would soon make—vital Qabalistic keys that unlocked fundamental mysteries of *The Book of the Law*[8] and the Aeon of Horus. Some of these were outlined in a tiny book, *Liber 31*[9] which Jones sent Crowley in 1919. Crowley couldn't be happier with the revelations; "Your key opens the Palace."[10]

---

6 *The Confessions of Aleister Crowley*, London, 1929. Abridged one-volume edition, edited by John Symonds and Kenneth Grant, London: 1969. Reprint London and New York: Arkana 1989, p. 801.
7 *Ibid.* p. 807.
8 Received by Aleister Crowley in 1904 E.V., *Liber AL vel Legis, The Book of the Law,* is the primary Holy Book of Thelema. It is found in numerous texts including *Liber ABA, Book Four.* 2d ed., Edited by Hymenaeus Beta, York Beach, Maine: Weiser Books, Inc., 1997, pp. 303–386.
9 Charles Stansfeld Jones, *Liber 31.* Edited and annotated by T. Allen Greenfield, Marietta, Georgia: Luxor Press, 1998.
10 *Ibid.* p. 2.

It seemed in Achad Crowley truly had found the "one" foretold in *The Book of the Law*; " . . . *the one to follow thee;*"[11] the one " . . . *who shall discover the Key of it all.* "[12]—the magical child and brilliant heir-apparent to the Great Beast and Prophet of the Aeon of Horus.

Perhaps he had. But the father-son relationship these two great adepts shared would not endure to the end. Eventually it would become strained to the breaking point, and amazingly, we know the exact day this beautiful relationship began to sour. We have a written record of the precise moment—the moment Frater Achad experienced either a quantum leap in consciousness, or else stepped off the zenith edge of supernal adeptship into the abyss of occult madness.[13]

It happened on May 31st, 1922 as Jones was writing the fourth chapter of *Q. B. L. or The Bride's Reception*—a moment that would literally turn the Qabalistic universe upside down.

"I had written thus far (May 31st, 1922 E.V.) when I was rewarded with the opening up of SECRETS so wonderful that they have changed my whole conception of the Plan of the Qabalah, and have indeed proved not alone a LIGHTNING FLASH to destroy THE HOUSE OF GOD but a SERPENT of WISDOM to reconstruct it, and yet again a STAR which explains all SYMBOLISM. This matter being of such TRANSCENDENT IMPORTANCE will be dealt with in the

---

11 *Liber AL vel Legis, The Book of the Law,* ch.1, vs.76.
12 *Ibid.* ch. .III, vs 47.
13 We must not dismiss the possibility that, from our below-the-abyss point of view, these two ideas might be in essence the same thing.

form of Appendixes to this Volume which will be obtainable under certain special conditions. Meanwhile the main plan of this book will be followed as originally intended, since it is necessary that the Student should have a clear and comprehensive grasp of the old system before he could appreciate the New."[14]

Fortunately for us, Jones did indeed follow the original plan of of the text through to completion and saved elucidations on his revolutionary theories for the book's Appendixes. This thoughtful gesture, in my opinion, renders the main text of *Q.B.L.* the clearest, most understandable, and practical introduction to the study of Qabalah written to that date. It also effectively prepares the more Qabalistically educated reader for the provocative ideas presented in the Appendixes—concepts that suggest that the traditional allocation of the letters of the Hebrew alphabet upon the 22 Paths of the Tree of Life should be in essence *reversed* in their positions.

Such a suggestion isn't necessarily heretical, especially when posited from the point of view of a Master of the Temple ($8° = 3^\square$), an adept whose consciousness abides above the Abyss that separates the Supernal Triad of the Tree of Life, (Kether-Chokmah-Binah)—an Abyss below which *division is the result of contradiction*, and above which *contradiction is unity*.

Crowley, however, was not impressed with what he considered to be Achad's flawed and immature grasp of this "rule of Contraries." He would later write,[15]

---

14 See page 47 of this text.
15 *Liber 418—The Vision & The Voice—with Commentary and Other Papers.* Aleister Crowley, York Beach, Maine: Weiser Books, Inc., 1998, p. 226.

"But this rule must be applied with skill and discretion, if error is to be avoided. It is a lamentable fact that worthy Zelator of A∴ A., one Frater Achad, having been taught (patiently enough) by the Seer to use this formula, was lured by his vanity to suppose that he had discovered it himself, and proceeded to apply it indiscriminately. He tried to stand the Serpent of Wisdom on its head, and argued that as he was a ($1° = 10^\square$), of the Order, he must equally be a ($10° = 1^\square$)! As The Book of Lies [chap. 63][16] says, "I wrenched DOG backwards to find God; now God barks!" He would have been better advised to reverse his adored ONE and taken a dose of ENO!"

("ONE" in Hebrew is "Achad." "ENO" is the brand name of an English laxative.)

A year later, in 1923 upon receipt of Achad's next book, *The Egyptian Revival*, Crowey voiced in his diary his exasperation with the direction his "son" was taking.

"What line shall I take with regard to Frater Achad's books? (I have just received The Egyptian Revival & a threat of others.) The point is this —the books—even apart from the absurd new attribution proposed for the Paths—are so hopelessly bad in almost every way—English, style, sense, point of view, oh everything! —yet they may do good to people they are written for. My real concern is lest he

---

16 *The Book of Lies* by Aleister Crowley, York Beach, Maine: Weiser Books, 1992, p. 136.

get too much ubris [Hubris] and come a real cropper."[17]

His fears become (at least in Crowley's mind) a reality. He wrote in *Magick in Theory and Practice*,[18]

"One who ought to have known better tried to improve the Tree of Life by turning the Serpent of Wisdom upside down! Yet he could not even make his scheme symmetrical: his little remaining good sense revolted at the supreme atrocities. Yet he succeeded in reducing the whole Magical Alphabet to nonsense, and shewing that he had never understood its real meaning.

"The absurdity of any such disturbance of the arrangement of the Paths is evident to any sober student from such examples as the following. Binah, the Supernal Understanding, is connected with Tiphereth, the Human Consciousness, by Zain, Gemini, the Oracles of the Gods, or the Intuition. That is, the attribution represents a psychological fact: to replace it by The Devil is either humour or plain idiocy. Again, the card "Fortitude," Leo, balances Majesty and Mercy with Strength and Severity: what sense is there in putting "Death," the Scorpion, in its stead? There are twenty other mistakes in the new wonderful illuminated-from-on-high attribution; the

---

17 *The Magical Diaries of Aleister Crowley,* ed. Stephen Skinner, Jersey: Neville Spearman and New York: Weiser Books, 1979, p. 127.
18 *Liber ABA, Book Four.* 2d ed., edited by Hymenaeus Beta, York Beach, Maine: Weiser Books, Inc., 1997.

student can therefore be sure of twenty more laughs if he cares to study it."[19]

But tell us how you really feel Mr. Crowley!

Of course, it can be argued that Crowley was simply jealous of Achad's discoveries, the speed of his initiatory advancement, and his independent spirit. After all, Crowley could be viciously cruel and petty. It must be pointed out, however, that no matter how bitterly he railed against Jones' new doctrines he always acknowledged and praised his role as the discoverer of the Qabalistic key to *Liber AL vel Legis, The Book of the Law.*

The fact remains that Jones' behavior as the years progressed lead many to believe that he suffered bouts of mental illness. Such things are hard to prove, especially where magicians are concerned, and should not necessarily cast negative aspersions upon the quality of his work done during healthier times, or negate the real possibility such behavior manifested because Jones was enraptured in inscrutably high levels of consciousness.

Yes, he would join the Roman Catholic Church in an attempt to transmute this world religion into one that accepts the Law of Thelema and the formula of the Age of Horus. But was that an act of insanity or simply the bold and audacious act of a Thelemic hero? Yes, he would be put away for flinging aside his raincoat to expose his nakedness to the masses of Vancouver. But are the naked Sadhus of India imprisoned for indecency?

It is easy for us (especially those of us whose initiatory careers place us conspicuously low on the Tree of Life) to point to these incidents and speculate how Achad's premature advance to Master of the Temple

---

19 *Ibid.* p. 141.

caused his ultimate fall into the madness of Daäth (the false Sephira, "Knowledge" that resides in the Abyss itself) to become a Black Brother. In truth, very few people on the face of the earth are qualified to make that judgment. Certainly not I.

Achad himself, however, gives us a chilling hint of his thoughts on this matter in a 1948 letter to Gerald Yorke.

> "If this New Æon is what it seems to be, it
> will have lifted the Curse of the Magus and
> destroyed the Glamour and Lies and Madness
> of the Supernal Paths. That would leave one
> in Daäth—and represent real Attainment—the
> becoming one with Those Who Know."[20]

Speculation and controversy aside, Frater Achad remains one of the most interesting and important magical figures of the 20th century. His initial Qabalistic discoveries continue to yield new and provocative ideas concerning *The Book of the Law* and other Holy Books of Thelema. Most exciting, in my opinion, is work currently under way on development of a Qabalah based upon the letters of the English alphabet,[21] which, while not an Achad "discovery" per se, is based in part on his *Liber 31*.

Q. B. L. or The Bride's Reception is a masterpiece of Qabalah and controversy. Its importance to the world

---

20 Jones, letter to Gerald Yorke, April, 1948.
21 "New Aeon English Qabala" Discovered by Jim Lees in 1976, the concept has been further developed by Jake Stratton-Kent, Carol Smith and members of Hermetic Alchemical Order of the QBLH (qblh@qblh.org). Also recommended —Gerald del Campo's, New Aeon English Qabalah Revealed, Marietta, Georgia: Luxor Press, 2003, and John Crow's, New Aeon English Qabalah Dictionary, Marietta, Georgia: Luxor Press, 2003.

of modern occult literature can be measured not only by its value as a remarkably understandable textbook of the fundamental principles of Qabalah, but also because it offers us a rare glimpse into the heart and mind of a brilliant and sincere seeker of wisdom and truth.

The Serpent Tongue

Liber 187

FOREWORD FOR THE 2011 EDITION[1]

There may be a certain amount of truth in the adage, "You can't teach an old dog new tricks." But for this old dog the English Qaballa[2] may very well be the most important new trick I will ever learn.

I suppose I can't be condemned too severely for taking so long to examine this marvelous spiritual instrument. After all, I have spent the better part of my adult life shunning those *centres of pestilence* who dared discuss or interpret the contents of *Liber AL vel Legis*.[3] I was especially distrustful of the poor souls who, in exchange for a coronation ceremony and the deed to certain real estate in Scotland, were prepared to assume the mantle of spiritual leadership of the world. Indeed, by 1983 my

---

1 Written for Jake Stratton-Kent. *The Serpent Tongue: Liber 187,* London: Hadean Press, 2011.

2 Alternate spellings; Qabala, Qabalah, Cabala, Kabbalah.

3 The Class A Comment on Liber AL vel Legis reads:
Do what thou wilt shall be the whole of the Law.
The study of this Book is forbidden. It is wise to destroy this copy after the first reading.
Whosoever disregards this does so at his own risk and peril. These are most dire. Those who discuss the contents of this Book are to be shunned by all, as centres of pestilence.
All questions of the Law are to be decided only by appeal to my writings, each for himself.
There is no law beyond Do what thou wilt.
Love is the law, love under will.
The priest of the princes,
Ankh-f-n-khonsu / [666]

collection of letters from individuals revealing themselves to be the incarnation of Aleister Crowley, or the "one to follow," or "... his child & that strangely ..." or the child of somebody's bowels," rivaled that of Dr. Regardie.[4] Indeed, shortly before his death the dear man and I even entertained the idea of pooling our letters and communications in a book called Liber Nutz.

The authors of nearly every one of these colorful documents claimed to have "cracked the code" of *The Book of the Law* and as proof offered elaborate explanations of the string of numbers and letters (words) that begin the 76th verse of the Second Chapter of *Liber AL vel Legis*:

4 6 3 8 A B K 2 4 A L G M O R 3 Y X 24 89 R P ST O V A L.

For example: the father of one "one to follow" was named Kenneth. The Hebrew word for father being "AB" it was perfectly obvious that ABK referred to his father—whose address at the time of the nativity of his child (& that strangely) was 4637 GILMORE ST. But, owing to phenomena arising from the obliquity of the earth's axis between 1904 and the date of his birth, the actual coordinates of his birth were shifted to just across the street at 4638. "What more proof could you want?" he asked. I didn't answer, but I did call Regardie and shared the story. We laughed like schoolyard bullies.

Today I am somewhat ashamed of my arrogant dismissals of what I now see as sincere and poignant pleas for spiritual validation from seekers who were

---

4   Francis Israel Regardie (née Regudy; 1907–1985) occultist, writer, and one-time personal secretary to Aleister Crowley.

desperately trying far better than I to apply the complex and colorful mythos of Thelema directly to their own lives. At the time, however, my cynicism hardened with each new revelation and so did my disdain for these still-born prophets with their roaring narcissism, delusions of grandeur, defective Hebrew, disjointed gematria, faulty arithmetic, poor command of the English language, and the utter incapacity to grasp the fact that whoever read their letters would immediately conclude they were mad as hatters.

Like most Thelemites, I did my own share of puttering. In the late 70s I took three yellow legal pads and determined the numeration for each word of *Liber AL*. I did this in a very orthodox manner by treating each English letter as its Hebrew counterpart(s). This was a singularly unsatisfying project. I was perpetually frustrated with uncertainties—uncertainty over whether or not this "t" is Tau or a Teth; or if that "x" is a Tzaddi or a Cheth, or of that "o" is a Vau or an Ayin. Despair followed frustration when my wife, Constance, (who hates the Qabalah) continually pummeled me with the obvious fact that *Liber AL* was not written in Hebrew so why on earth should the letters of its words be translated into Hebrew. My defense was feeble;

"For one reason," I explained to her with sweet condescension, "to see their relationships to significant traditional Qabalistic words and concepts." "And where do those words and concepts come from?" she asked. (She knew the answer. She was just being mean.)

"The Bible . . . mostly." I mumbled.

"Well, the Bible's not my Holy Book, and *The Book of the Law* doesn't need the Bible to prop it up! Show me a Qabalah in English . . . one that uses *The Book of the Law* and not the Bible!"

Of course, she was (and is always) right. I eventually abandoned this avenue of research and became, for the most part, contented to appeal exclusively to Crowley's writings for insights and inspiration. As far as exploring the English alphabet—I toyed half-heartedly with *Liber Trigrammaton* the same way a child pushes his broccoli around his plate, but that was it. I did, however, make one pathetic (yet remarkably successful) foray into *Liber AL* practical magick.

I projected the numbers and letters from II. 76 upon a kamea of Sol, thusly:

4 6 3 8 A B   K 2 4 A L   G M O R 3 Y   X 24
89   R P ST OV   A L

I printed it on gold/yellow card stock and laminated it in plastic. Our first test-run of this talisman was to see if it could help us find a new place to live. This may not sound like very serious magick, but if you've ever attempted to find a reasonably inexpensive house to lease in Newport Beach California then I'm afraid you don't really know the meaning of the words "impossible miracle." Our technique was simplicity itself. We taped the square to the dashboard of our car and drove around the neighborhood where we most desired to live. As rental rates in the new neighborhood were completely out of the price range we could afford, we wisely armed ourselves with a bottle of wine to assure we would not be dissuaded by common sense.

Without going into details (that are fascinating to us, but I'm sure are of little interest to the reader) I will simply report that in the ensuing twenty-five years we have needed to celebrate this ritual six times to locate new homes. It has always worked to the amazement of our neighbors and friends and to our own immense satisfaction.

I mention this magick square not to prove what a clever boy I was or to tout the power inherent in *The Book of the Law*. I bring it up only to point out the rather sad spiritual state into which I had allowed myself to drift. There I was, a hot-shot Thelemite. I militantly preached that *Liber AL vel Legis* was the revelatory instrument of the age. I studied it daily and supported that study by performing rituals based upon its deities and formulae; by reading, memorization, and meditation. I was the best damned *Book of the Law* thumper in town! But the most practical thing I had ever done with it was to concoct a crude talisman for house hunting! Hell! Why not just get a sun-bleached buffalo bone, scratch a few markings on it with a sharp stone, and hurl it at the moon?

Well, maybe I'm being a bit hard on myself. The young fool, having neither the wit to see the enormity of his ignorance, nor the good sense to forsake the quest, eventually grew to be an old fool. Don't get me wrong. I don't think I wasted a minute on my magical education. I may have early on abandoned my tinkering with the Chapter II, verse 76, but I did spend the next twenty-five years or so immersing myself in the words, images and concepts that form the building-blocks of the magnificent edifice that is Thelema.

I speak particularly of the treasures to be found in *Liber AL vel Legis* and the 13 *Holy Books*. What an absolute thrill it is, at this rather late point in my magical life, to finally get a glimpse of what certainly appears to me to be the mathematical mortar that unites these great scriptural stones. Please do not think that I am presuming to speak for anyone other than myself when I voice my comments in this place. I am not writing as a spokesperson for any of the fine organizations to which I belong, and whose kind forbearance suffer my membership. However, as an individual, I cannot hide my personal enthusiasm concerning the English Qaballa (based upon the ALWHS . . . etc. progression) and marvelous work being done by Jake Stratton-Kent and others who are continuing to develop and enrich it. They deserve the admiration and thanks of every student of modern magick.

Liber 187 is a particularly brilliant example how rituals and exercises can be created from this marvelous structure. After I read it for the first time I wrote Jake and told him "It's so clean, it squeaks!" It is indeed so clean it squeaks—English words and phrases relating to other English words and phrases—magick words—familiar words that course through the dynamic matrix of a small collection of spiritual literature that I personally hold sacred.

Perhaps an old dog can learn a new trick or two. I certainly intend to find out.

The Qabalah Workbook for Magicians

A Guide to the Sephiroth

Foreword for the 2013 Edition[1]

The Qabalah is not a belief system. It's a way of looking at things. It's a way of organizing your universe so neatly that you eventually discover your own place in it.

—Rabbi Lamed Ben Clifford[2]

I am an old hippie. In 1967, however, I was a *young* hippie. I had very long hair, dressed in colorful sweatshirts and karate pants. I went barefoot a lot. More importantly, I had enthusiastically embarked (with the aide of psychoactive chemicals and the works of Paramahansa Yogananda, Alan Watts, Dr. Timothy Leary, and Beatles) upon a journey of self-exploration and discovery that continues to this day.

The mid 1960s were a cosmic aberration—a crack in space-time. It was certainly a remarkable season of

---

1 Written for Anita Kraft, *The Qabalah Workbook for Magicians,* Newburyport, Massachusetts: Weiser Books, 2013.
2 Lon Milo DuQuette. *The Chicken Qabalah of Rabbi Lamed Ben Clifford,* York Beach, Maine: Weiser Books, 2001, p.150.

history; an exhilarating and magical age to be alive and young. In that golden moment it was possible for a shallow young bumpkin from Nebraska—possessed of no more intelligence or wisdom than a turnip—to stumble naively into the sanctum sanctorum of *Montsalvat,* and with cud-chewing nonchalance take a good long slurp from the Holy Grail. I came away from those early psychedelic experiences with the Technicolor realization that God is consciousness—consciousness is the secret of existence—consciousness is the secret of life—and that *I am consciousness.*

Mind-expanding drugs were just what was needed to blast open the heavily barricaded doors of my constipated and medieval perception, but once that gate was duly and truly breached I was faced with the fact that the obstacles that remained on my path would be far more subtle and difficult to remove. These occlusions would require the use of more delicate ordnance. For spiritual nutrients I grazed upon the obligatory classics of Buddhist and Hindu literature, and I graduated from drugs to the quiet disciplines of meditation and eastern mysticism. I cut my hair, went vegetarian and fancied myself a yogi.

Yes! I was all prepared to be a first-class eastern mystic—at least I thought that's where I was going. Something, however, just didn't seem right. On an intellectual level I had no difficulty grasping the mystical concept that I (my *real* self) was something profoundly more than my body and my thoughts and my emotions. I understood that my *real self* was in essence the perfect reflection of the absolute and Supreme Consciousness (that great "whatever-it-is" within which resides everything, and *of which* the manifested universe is just an expression). It was perfectly clear to me that if I could only strip away all the things that I was *not* then the only thing remaining would be exactly that! . . . *The Only Thing*—and that only thing would be both the Supreme Consciousness *and* me!

This, I concluded with youthful certainty was what eastern mystics were shooting for. This level of consciousness is the profound "nothingness" of Nirvana— the wall-to-wall totality of Samadhi. All I had to do was strip down to my most naked me—and when I got there my "I"-ness would disappear into the big "whatever-it-is"-ness of the Supreme Consciousness.

But alas, I was a very poor meditator. Oh, I could look like a pretty good meditator. I could sit still in my asana for long periods of time with a full teacup and saucer balanced on my head.[3] My skill in pranayama was admirable, and I could hold the clear image of working pendulum clock in my mind's eye for eternal micro-seconds at a time. But something was profoundly wrong with my work; and I'll wager that the astute reader has probably already identified exactly what was wrong with my view of this whole enlightenment business. Here . . . I'll say it for you . . .

"Mr. DuQuette, for a mystic you use the word 'I' an awful lot. Aren't you suppose to lose your ego as you near enlightenment?"

Bingo! Guilty as charged! I knew, of course, that eventually we must transcend identity with the ego to become the absolute Supreme Consciousness (just as we must transcend our identity with the *body* and the *emotions* and the *mind*). But for the life of me I couldn't remove the objective "me" in the subjective

---

3 Really! Ask Constance. She had to put that full teacup on my head each morning!

"dissolution-of-me" process. I couldn't shake the idea of how *cool* I was going *look* gaining enlightenment—how cool I was going to look with *no ego!*

At first I felt a little embarrassed about all this. But, as serious self-condemnation has never been one of my virtues, I soon came to the giddy realization that I was simply trying to play eastern software on my western hardware. Perhaps I was hardwired by nature and western civilization not to seek divine union by *stripping away* all the things I *am not*, but instead by *uniting* myself with all the things that *I am*. Profound *emptiness* and profound *fullness* are one-and-the-same. The disciplines of the east oblige the mystic to look inward for union with God; and that's great for the eastern, introspective disposition. The western psyche, on the other hand, is inclined to look outwards. We love scripture and ritual drama that gives outward expression to inward realities. In either case the supreme goal is the same. Which approach one takes is simply a matter of one's cultural temperament. I'm as western as they come. So I'm an "out-y."

I turned my attention to what the West might have to offer, and began my search for 'western software'—a western equivalent to the *Tao*—a western equivalent to *Zen*, and I more or less found what I was looking for in the Qabalah.

My introduction to the Qabalah was the indirect result of my youthful involvement with the Rosicrucian Order AMORC.[4] Encouraged by my older brother Marc, I had joined the Order in the early 1970s in hopes it would give me something spiritual and wholesome to occupy my nervous energy as I transitioned from the

---

4   AMORC. Ancient and Mystical Order Rosae Crucis, an international fraternal organization founded in 1915 by advertising executive Harvey Spencer Lewis and others.

recording artist's life of sex, drugs, and rock 'n' roll to the docility of a domesticated husband and father.

AMORC's monograph teachings were delivered promptly each week by mail and were an offbeat combination of solitary ritual meditations and Junior High science and chemistry experiments. Much as I had hated school I found the AMORC material oddly fascinating and inspiring. I was nothing short of ecstatic when I attended my first "convocation" service at a local lodge in Long Beach. I discovered then and there that I absolutely loved dressing up in spooky robes, intoning strange chants, and strutting around in the dark.

As I ascended up the degree structure of the organization I learned that certain mystical perks could be redeemed. I was informed by a fellow member that when I reached a certain degree level I would qualify to order and receive additional monograph instructions in certain mystically related subjects. One such extracurricular monograph series was on "The Holy Kabbalah," and I impatiently awaited the time when I would be qualified to register for the teachings. When that day finally arrived I sent off a money order for the course and eagerly awaited my initiation into the mysteries of the Holy Kabbalah.

The six monographs arrived in one envelope and I read all six in one sitting. There was the brief historical sketch and a bibliography, but no meditations, no rituals, or exercises. Indeed, there was nothing that made any sense to me at all. In fact, most of the text was filled with dire warnings to the student about what the Kabbalah is *not*. I cannot resist satirically paraphrasing:

Kabbalah is spelled "Kabbalah." If you run across literature that spells it with only one "B" it is not really Kabbalah and you should run away from it. If you run across literature that spells it with a "Q" or a "C" or indeed in any way other than "Kabbalah" it is not real Kabbalah and you should stop reading and run away.

Kabbalah is not something that is written down so don't expect to discover anything about it by reading stuff. Kabbalah is only passed orally from one pious Jewish man over the age of 40 but under 80, who is rich enough to have a lot of leisure time to devote to studying Kabbalah, to another Jewish man over the age of 40 but under 80 who is also rich enough to have a lot of leisure time to devote to studying Kabbalah.

Kabbalah has nothing to do with a diagram called the Tree of Life. . . . If you see a Tree of Life . . . run away! Kabbalah has nothing to do with the Tarot Cards. . . . If you see Tarot cards . . . run away! Kabbalah has nothing to do with magic . . . If you see anything to do with magic . . . run away!

Kabbalah is the secret, esoteric, hidden, forbidden, furtive, and most likely *dangerous* study of the Holy Bible and it is certainly not for presumptuous young dilettantes like *you*. In fact you should be embarrassed for even being curious as to what Kabbalah might be about.

Thank you for waiting two years for these
monographs and for sending $15.00.
Now . . . RUN AWAY![5]

That was in 1972. Things have changed in the world of Qabalah! Kabbalah, Cabala, Qabalah is everywhere; books, lessons, teachings, organizations, even videos, movies, and CDs can be purchased, attended, viewed and listened to whenever you like. What remains a rarity, however, are competent, practical instructions as to how to actually incorporate the fundamentals of Qabalah into one's daily life and routine. For me it has been a hit and miss comedy of errors and accidental triumphs, and perhaps that's how it should always be. But it is clear to me that the work needn't be harder on the poor student than absolutely necessary.

How can today's serious student actually begin the process of inoculating himself or herself with the virus of qabalistic thought—that divine dis-ease that eventually incubates in the soul and hatches as illumination? How does a modern mystic go about connecting everything in the universe with everything else until there is no "anything else" left?

In an attempt to answer those questions I wrote a little book that I whimsically called, *The Chicken Qabalah*[6]. It was quite frankly the text I wished I could have read when I first began my Qabalah adventure. Over the years the book has been well received, and for the most part I am satisfied that my labor has been

---

5   Of course I'm exaggerating. I have the greatest respect for the organization, and except for this outrageously discouraging set of monographs have nothing but wonderful memories of my AMORC experiences.
6   Lon Milo DuQuette. *The Chicken Qabalah of Rabbi Lamed Ben Clifford*, Newburyport, Massachusetts: Weiser Books. 2001.

rewarded. I am especially gratified that it was chosen by Ms. Anita Kraft as one of the source books for her marvelous *Qabalah Workbook for Magicians*. Her work is that rarest of magical tools, an elegant, hands-on course in practical Qabalah. A book that obliges you to roll up your sleeves and do things with the Qabalah. I am particularly thrilled because reading her book has afforded me the opportunity to witness a new generation of qabalistic magician whose brilliance shines not only from the fact that she "gets it" in the traditional sense, but also because she is pushing the technology forward in fresh, innovative, and exhilarating ways. I am proud to be in a small measure associated with its publication.

In closing I would like to leave you with the last seventy-two words uttered my favorite Qabalah teacher and (until his mysterious disappearance a few years ago) our family's life-long spiritual counselor, Rabbi Lamed Ben Clifford. The dear man once told me, "Ron"—he never could remember my name—" Ron, the Qabalah is not a belief system. It's a way of looking at things. It's a way of organizing your universe so neatly that you eventually discover your own place in it."

It is my sincerest wish that this little book will aid and comfort you as you organize *your* universe so neatly that you will eventually discover your own place in it.

Bless you all. Shalom.

THE SECRET OF THE SHEM-HA MEPHORASH
The Last Written Words of Rabbi Lamed Ben Clifford[7]

God is.

Undivided God is pure potentiality and realizes Nothing.

God can only realize Itself by becoming Many and then experiencing all possibilities through the adventures of Its many parts.

The ultimate purpose for My existence is to exhaust My individual potentiality.

My Love of God and God's love of Me springs from the Great Secret we share.

The Secret is

God and I will achieve Supreme Enlightenment at the same moment.

7 Lon Milo DuQuette. *The Chicken Qabalah of Rabbi Lamed Ben Clifford,* York Beach Maine: Weiser Books, 2001, p. 202.

The Secret Language of Tarot

Afterword to the 2008 Edition[1]

As a young man I was introduced to tarot as an adjunct to my study of Rosicrucianism and the Hermetic Qabalah.[2] It was never my intention to use the cards as a divinatory tool (an activity frowned upon by the mystery "school" I attended through a correspondence course). Indeed, I was counseled that if I were to use the cards to tell fortunes it would cripple me spiritually. I took my teachers at their word and proceeded for the next three years to use the cards for meditation purposes only.

Part of the school's curriculum was the requirement that each student paint his or her own deck of tarot cards trumps. The course provided an unpainted deck of the 22 trumps bearing clean black outlines of the figures on each card and very strict coloring instructions. Each card took two weeks to color during which time certain texts and meditations were assigned. I must admit that at the end of forty-four weeks I knew every detail of the cards.

The mystical power inherent in the images was apparent from the first weeks of my study. The evening I completed coloring *The Fool* would become one of the

1 Written for Ruth Ann and Wald Amberstone *The Secret Language of Tarot*, York Beach, Maine: Weiser Books, 2008.

2 The "Hermetic Qabalah" is a facet of the Hebrew Kabbalah embraced and utilized by students of magick and the Western Mystery traditions.

most memorable of nights of my life. During the night I experienced the most marvelous vision. It was unlike anything I had ever experienced (even in the 60s!). It was so intense that even after I woke up and turned on the light, the living images continued to play across the screen of my vision.

I won't bore you with the curiously personal details of this nocturnal initiation. It is enough to say that it *was* an initiation—not an initiation into the bricks and mortar "order" that mailed me my monographs each week, but into the "temple" of tarot itself. I knew without a shadow of doubt that my two weeks with *The Fool* card had reprogrammed my psyche and triggered a glimpse of a higher lever of consciousness. What would become of me when I finished the whole deck? I thought.

Now, over thirty years later, tarot continues to play a central role in my life. It is my constant companion. Its perfect Qabalistic structure and construction is a constant source of wonder and illumination. It is the spyglass, counselor, and commentator of an examined life, and I view the streaming events of my ever-changing existence as the shuffling, spreading, and reshuffling of the cards. My relationship with the cards has long ago transcended the stage of, *"Oh my! The damned Prince of Cups is beating me with the 3 of Disks again."* The cards have ceased to be metaphoric cartoons of my intellect and reasoning process, and have literally become communicating angels of my intuitional life. In the language of tarot I am moving from the world of Swords to the world of Cups, and tarot gives me the secret language, the vocabulary to voice such ineffable spiritual subtleties. That is perhaps tarot's greatest gift to the student of the soul—the ability to communicate with the various parts of our being—to give form and meaning to parts of our psyche that are formless and indefinable. The secret language. The gift of the god Thoth.

I've long since abandoned my eschewing of tarot as a divinatory tool. This is not to say that I consider my readings for other people to be a form of fortunetelling. Tarot, or indeed any oracle, cannot show us the future or directly answer our questions. Tarot is simply vehicle of perfection, and eternal truth is revealed in perfection. Used with proper attention such oracles serve to announce the status not of the future, but of the *Great Now*. It's the person who consults the oracle who must somehow glimpse the future or hear the answer to his or her question in that announcement.

That being said, I can honestly say that I have never consciously made an important decision based upon information I've received from a tarot reading (especially my own) or any other form of divination. This is not because I don't have confidence in the wisdom and efficacy of oracles, but because I am a self-centered, self-involved, bull-headed old fool who seldom takes wise advice from any of his friends or family, let alone from a pack of cards or the role of the dice.

I *have*, however, encountered adepts whose tarot insights are eminently worthy of decision-making counsel. Two of them, in fact, are the authors of this book for which I am proud to pen this brief Foreword. The Amberstones are dear friends (I officiated at their wedding.) and directors of one of the most respected tarot schools in the world. Their tarot credentials are impeccable, but their greatest qualification to speak with authority on this sacred subject is the fact they comfortably embody in their lives a conspicuous level of balance, wisdom and sanity. In short, they are walking examples of lives illuminated through contact and mastery of the secret *language of tarot*.

Tarot and Psychology

Spectrums of Possibility

Promise me never to abandon the sexual theory.
That is the most essential thing of all. You see, we
must make a dogma of it, an unshakable bulwark
. . . against the black tide of mud . . . of occultism.

—Freud writing to Jung, 1913

I knew that I would never be able to accept such an
attitude. What Freud seemed to mean by "occultism"
was virtually everything that philosophy and reli-
gion, including the rising contemporary science of
parapsychology, had learned about the psyche.

—Jung's reaction to Freud's statement

For at least five centuries the Tarot has tenaciously survived the condemnation of church, the persecution of
state and the ridicule of academia. Long the instrument
of fortune-tellers and persons of dubious if not feloni-
ous character, the Tarot enters the new millennium still
in the guise of a fallen angel. However, unlike Milton's

---

1   Written for Arthur Rosengarten PhD, *Tarot and Psychology: Sprectrums of Possibility,* Vadnais Heights, Minnesota: Paragon House, 2000.

rebellious protagonist, the Tarot now hovers dangerously close to redemption. I am pleased, but not at all surprised, to learn that these ancient and evocative images are now attracting the serious attention of modern mental health professionals. Foremost among this is Arthur Rosengarten, PhD whose provocative and thoroughly readable work is the subject of these brief words.

Since the mid-nineteenth century, adepts of Western Hermeticism have attempted to demonstrate that the Tarot is constructed in strict conformity with the fundamental principles of Hebrew mysticism known as the Kabbalah. They asserted that images of the Tarot, especially those displayed on the 22 trump cards, are visual personifications of various aspects of Deity which had been categorized with anal retentive zeal by unnamed Hebrew sages at some time in the distant past.

The ancient Hebrew philosophers built upon the scriptural premise that Man was created in the image of God. Later esotericists, observing the phenomena of repeating patterns in nature, and remembering the Hermetic axiom "as above, so below," tended to agree, albeit with less parochial bias. They reasoned that if the images of the Tarot were metaphors of aspects of divine consciousness then, it followed, they also must be reflected on the human level as key components of the psyche—archetypal citizens of the mind which each of us share with our fellows.

While I do not presume to speak with any measure of authority on matters relating to the field of psychology, I do feel somewhat qualified to speak on matters touching on Kabbalah and Tarot. It is clear to me that the "mystical" concept of the archetypal images of the Tarot is identical in essence with those of Jung's Universal

Collective Unconscious. Moreover, I firmly believe that under certain circumstances the images of the Tarot can trigger, activate, subdue, direct, or empower the specific dynamics these archetypes represent.

Regrettably, few professionals are aware of the practical potential of the Tarot. Fewer still are as yet willing to risk the condemnation of colleagues by embarking upon a course of study that would enable them to skillfully employ this tool in a therapeutic environment. A master of both disciplines, Dr. Rosengarten remains somewhat immune to such concerns. He is a pioneer in the purest sense of the word. Not only has he courageously ventured into uncharted territory, he has lingered along the way to break ground and erect landmarks for the benefit of those who will inevitably follow.

Ironically, the antagonism, real or imagined, that exists between the Tarot and Psychology parallels in many respects the fundamental differences between Eastern and Western mysticism. The Eastern mystic, by tradition (and perhaps because of temperament), is taught to quietly plunge inwardly to meet the myriad facets of self of their own turf. Furthermore, to overcome the distractions of mind which hinder this inner self-communion, he or she strives with ruthless meditative fervor to virtually assassinate the harpies of thought, creating as it were a vacuum into which pure illumination will theoretically pour.

The Western mind, on the other hand, prefers to deal objectively with subjective matters. We want to reach in, personify them, pull them out, throw them down in front of us and have it out with them here and now. But dealing objectively with internal realities is impossible if one is unable to recognize and engage them as such. For what more perfect tool could one ask than a deck of colorful archetypal images that can me manipulated at will in nearly infinite combination. As the author points out:

> In a typical ten card spread, the chances of reproducing an exact duplication are simply staggering when one calculates the probability from a deck of 78 highly differentiated cards. But with Tarot, a transpersonal commonality is equally brought to bear upon human individuality and difference. This perhaps is why Tarot's light shines through all quadrants of the psychological universe and may be applicable in varying degrees to diverse theoretical persuasions.

> The symbolic language of Tarot compacts multiple levels of meaning into each card illustration and synchronistically one soon learns that there are no accidents in Tarot (or life), or put differently, accidents themselves are inherently meaningful. Universal themes of human experience unfold within original permutation of the Tarot matrix, reflecting countless variation on common myths, such as the perennial stages of human suffering and attainment, the psychological tasks and demand of human development, and the mysteries and potentials of the human spirit.

Rosengarten's landmark work spans the abyss that yawns between psychology and mysticism. Remarkably, it does so without diminishment to either art or science; indeed, both are immeasurably enriched by his unique contributions. It is obvious that this is a work written primarily for the continuing education of mental health professionals. (Certainly its meticulous notes, exhaustive references, bibliography and heroic index set it apart from nearly every book on Tarot ever published.) Nevertheless, we of the Tarot/metaphysical community should welcome it with particular gratitude and interest for it offers us a rare and entirely new look at an ancient tradition.

Music of the Tarot

LINER NOTES FOR THE 1998 ALBUM[1]

For centuries the beautiful and mysterious images of the Tarot have captivated the imagination of Western Civilization. The earliest examples date from the 14th Century and (it is commonly believed) were introduced to Europe by nomadic Gypsies who used the 78 cards as a fortune-telling device. But, as modern students have discovered, the Tarot is much more than a parlor game; it is a living, evolving pictorial storybook of the Divine. The entire deck is structured and organized in concordance with the ancient principles of the Hebrew Qabalah. Each card not only represents a Divine aspect of nature, but visually triggers the corresponding psychic center in the human consciousness.

MAJOR ARCANA (The Trumps)

Part 1: The Fool through The Lovers

Divine wisdom is foolishness to we mortals. What made the pre-existent Absolute forsake the perfect bliss of Nothingness in order to initiate creation? We cannot answer. We only know that the Universe springs from the Great Zero. Appropriately, our odyssey begins as a babe in a blue egg; or a handsome young **Fool**, neither male

---

1 Written for David and Richard Gordon, *Music of the Tarot*, Sequoia Records, 1998.

nor female gazing guilelessly into the sky before stepping off a precipice into a vast abyss. Tumbling through the void, the Fool becomes the All, and is transformed into a progression of archetypal characters and images.

As the **Magus**, the All has become the self-conscious, directed, concentrated Will. This Cosmic Magician functions as a conduit, transferring that which is above to that which is below. The weapons of his magick are: the Wand with which he creates; the Cup with which he preserves; the Dagger with which he destroys; and the Disk with which he redeems the world. His counterpart is the **High Priestess**. Only the Virginal Goddess of eternity is worthy to become the Great Mother of Fertility. Her chaste truth is of such purity that it can be veiled only by undulating waves of Light. As the Magus is the Will of creation, the High Priestess is the idea.

The union of the Magus and the High Priestess transforms them both; she into the **Empress**, the Great Mother Goddess, gate of all life; and he into the **Emperor**, Lord of patriarchal power, imperious director of energy. His marriage to the Empress is of primary importance to the governance of the cosmos, for their child, the **Hierophant**, will unite the Macrocosm (the world of the Gods) with the Microcosm (the world of humanity). He is the "God-Man," symbol of human evolution in the New Age; when each of us must be responsible for our own spiritual destiny. That which is above is united and harmonized in each individual with that which is below. "There is no bond that can unite the divided but love"; in **The Lovers** card, all of the previous Tarot characters achieve their synthesis. Ecstasy dissolves the illusion of separateness; through the thundering silence comes the Oracle of the Gods.

MAJOR ARCANA (The Trumps)

Part 2: The Chariot through Art

Riding as a triumphant king, the Knight of the Holy Graal conveys the precious secret of life in a starry, canopied **Chariot**. The blood is the life, cosmic equivalent of evolving DNA, carried by the Charioteer through the sea of infinite generations.

The process of creation finds the perfect partner in the manifest Goddess of **Adjustment** (Justice). With her golden scales she equilibrates all energies, forces, and principles; against the feather of her perfect truth she weighs the heart of humanity.

The **Hermit** stands upon his lonely mountaintop and gives his light to the world. It is also he who descends into the underworld of our subconscious and, if we allow him, will guide us to the celestial heavens of super-consciousness. From this spiritual vantage we see the cyclic nature of creation, an ever changing, ever increasing, ever diminishing **Wheel of Fortune**. The power, which turns the wheel, is the primal, undirected **Lust** (Strength) of solar energy, symbolized by a beautiful Goddess astride a great lion. It is she who now bears the Holy Graal.

The still, blue waters that suspend the Fool as a babe, serve also to reflect. Is it you, or is it the **Hanged Man** who is upside down? His self-sacrifice is not an occasion for mourning. **Death** is life itself. The caterpillar dies to become the butterfly; the maiden dies to become the mother. Without the Great Transformer there can be no new beginnings.

A royal marriage, the alchemical union of opposites is celebrated in the **Art** (Temperance) card. Male and Female, Sun and Moon are conjoined to create the elixir of life. Fire is poured upon water and water upon fire to produce the rainbow seal of a Divine covenant.

MAJOR ARCANA (The Trumps)

Part 3: The Devil through The Universe

All matter is born from the blending of Darkness and Light. The fearsome appearance of the **Devil** projects the illusion that we are hopelessly enmeshed in material existence. But the material world is our school; not our prison. Ignorance and superstition are the true "devils" that would bind the human spirit. So long as our eyes are closed, we remain in darkness. Old fears and attitudes must be destroyed like lightning struck **Tower**. Once illusion is annihilated, true meditation can begin. Illumination arises within like the evening **Star**.

Like images in our dreams, the **Moon** is a portrait of our shifting unconscious. She appears to shine, but merely reflects the light; she appears to change shape, yet that is only her ever changing position to the **Sun**, the true symbol of Life, Light, Love and Liberty. Our ancestors, in their ignorance, saw the Sun as a dying God, sacrificed daily and yearly only to resurrect each morning and each spring. So deeply ingrained was this image, that we believed ourselves also subject to death . . . a death that required continual elaborate rituals to assure our "life-after-death." In older Tarot decks this process was portrayed in the card entitled The Last Judgment. With the new **Aeon**, however, has come the dawn of new consciousness. We know the Sun does not die, nor does it need to be resurrected. Night, winter and death are all illusions . . . a simple shifting of a shadow. Our spiritual identity has now shifted from the Earth to the Sun. As such, we close the cycle of Trumps by taking our proper place in the **Universe**, dancing like the divine Fool in the center of the belt of the Zodiac, ready to withdraw, once again, into Nothingness.

MINOR ARCANA (The Four Suits)

The ancient Qabalists divided creation into four descending levels. Every aspect of Deity has its proper place within the fourfold structure, including the celestial personages such as Seraphim, Cherubim, Archangels, Angels, and yes, even human beings. In the Tarot, the four suits represent the four Elemental Worlds: **Wands** (Fire), **Cups** (Water), **Swords** (Air) and **Disks** (Earth). Within each suit is a **Knight**, a **Queen**, a **Prince** and a **Princess**, who represent respectively the fiery, watery, airy and earthly aspects of each suit. In addition to these "Court" cards, each suit has ten numbered cards; the Ace is the archetypal emblem of the suit, and Two through Ten expose the dynamic inner workings of the element.

> **WANDS** (Fire): Representing the highest of the four worlds, the Wands symbolize the fiery Will of the God, source of all energy and creative passion. **Dominion** (2); **Virtue** (3); **Completion** (4); **Strife** (5); **Victory** (6); **Valor** (7); **Swiftness** (8); and **Strength** (9) finally degenerate into **Oppression** (10) as we descend the ladder of the world of Wands.

> **CUPS** (Water): As water both mirrors and absorbs light, the suit of Cups receives the

influence of the Wands and reflects and nurtures their radiance. This is the heart and Soul of God. **Love** (2); **Abundance** (3); **Luxury** (4); **Disappointment** (5); **Pleasure** (6); **Debauch** (7); **Indolence** (8); and **Happiness** (9); dissolve uneasily into **Satiety** (10) as the work of Water is completed.

SWORDS (Air): A sword slashing through the air can destroy, defend, discriminate, enforce judgment and invoke powers either for good or for evil. What better symbol for the for the perpetually all-creative Mind of God? Even the titles of the suit of Swords sing of the triumphs and tragedies of the mind. **Peace** (2); **Sorrow** (3); **Truce** (4); **Defeat** (5); **Science** (6); **Futility** (7); **Interference** (8); and **Cruelty** (9); end inevitably in **Ruin** (10); if reason ignores the influence of the will and the heart.

DISKS (Earth): Disks represent the manifested material plane, lowest of the four worlds and visible fruit of their influence. Money is a perfect example of the Disk; it is a coin, the reward of physical labor (Disks), which is directed by intellectual processes (Swords), which has been inspired by creative visualization (Cups) and motivated by the will to achieve (Wands). All things on the material plane are the product of this fourfold development. **Change** (2); **Work** (3); **Power** (4); **Worry** (5); **Success** (6); **Failure** (7); **Prudence** (8); **Gain** (9); and finally **Wealth**

(10); rewards the courageous traveler at the end
of our Tarot journey.

But the journey has not really ended. The *Tarot*,
often spelled *Taro*, is not a ladder, but a wheel . . . a *Rota*
. . . a helix, a snake swallowing its tail; perpetually beginning anew as a Great Zero.

From the Divine Nothingness of the *Fool* to the
infinite *Wealth* of the 10 of Disks—the sequence repeats
itself through eternity—for is it not a Great Truth that a
Fool and his *Money* are soon parted?

PART FOUR

THELEMIC MAGICK

~~~~~~~~~~~~~~~~~~~~~~~~~~

the Law is for all.
Do what thou wilt shall be the whole of the Law.
Love is the law, love under will.

Behold! the rituals of the old time are black. Let the
evil ones be cast away; let the good ones be purged by
the prophet! Then shall this Knowledge go aright.

The Kabbalah, Magick, and Thelema

Selected Writings Vol. II

INTRODUCTION TO THE 2005 EDITION[1]

Do what thou wilt shall be the whole of the Law.

I met her first in the fog-shrouded early morning hours of November 15, 1975 EV at a motel in Dublin, California. I had traveled all night by bus from Costa Mesa. It had not been a restful journey. All I could think about for every bumpy mile was the initiation I was scheduled to undergo and the curious circumstance that brought me to this moment in my life.

It had taken nearly two years of handwritten letters back and forth . . . letters demanding the location, date and hour of my birth, my biography, my education, my aspirations. Finally, a date was set for my initiation, and my instructions were clear, simple, and utterly terrifying.

As the bus neared Dublin I was to tell the driver I wanted to be let off at a particular intersection near a certain motel. I was to walk a few blocks to the motel and check in using my own name. If there were no rooms available I was to wait in the lobby. If there was a room available I was

---

1 Written for Phyllis Seckler (Soro Meral), edited by Dr. David Shoemaker, Gregory Peters, and Rorac Johnson, *The Kabbalah, Magick, and Thelema: Selected Writings Vol. II*, York, Maine: The Teitan Press, 2005.

to go there and wait to be contacted. I had no other information—no address—no phone number—I didn't even know the names of my hosts and initiators, only magical names: *Hymenaeus Alpha, 777,* and *Soror Meral.*

As I looked out the bus window at the cold moon rising over the abyss that is the San Joaquin Valley it occurred to me that should I fall victim of foul play—should I vanish from off the face of the earth—if my initiators were the insane remnants of some Satanic Aleister Crowley cannibal cult—should they choose to rape me, kill me, and eat me (something I was not completely convinced was not part of the program) my poor wife wouldn't even have a clue to give the police.

I didn't know it at the time, but Hymenaeus Alpha and Soror Meral were having their own doubts and fears about me, and that the reason for all the cloak and dagger dramatics was the very real concern that *I* might be a dangerous person. In the months prior to my initial inquiry note some very scary things had taken place in California. The homes of several prominent people, elderly former students of Aleister Crowley, had been burgled and their priceless collection of Crowley books and magical articles stolen.

The neon sign in front of the motel beamed a welcoming "Vacancy" and shortly after I awakened the poor manager and checked in I found myself stretched out comfortably on top of a not-so-hard bed. I immediately fell asleep and dreamed the most disturbing dream . . . of saggy-titted old women with poorly-dyed red hair, and priapic old Englishmen in goat leggings carving up my raped and murdered body and devouring my limbs with mint sauce.

"Lon!"

I heard a woman's voice distinctly and forcefully calling out my name. I woke up and jumped off the bed. "Coming!" I shouted through the door. I tidied my shirt a bit and popped a mint in my mouth and opened the door. There was no one there. I stepped out and looked in both directions . . . no one there.

Somewhat shaken, I returned to my room and sat down on the edge of the bed. Things were starting to get uncomfortably magical. I heard that voice as loudly and as clearly as if someone were standing right outside the door. I was hesitant to try to go back to sleep but eventually stretched out again. As soon as my head hit the pillow the phone rang—irritatingly loud. I picked up before it could wound my ears a second time.

"Hello," I answered, almost as a question.

"Lon DuQuette?" It was the voice of the woman who *wasn't* at the door. By now I wasn't surprised at anything that was happening.

"Yes."

"Have you eaten?"

She didn't sound like a cannibal.

"No." I admitted. "Have you?"

About a half an hour later a knock on my door told me a flesh and blood Soror Meral was on the threshold. When I opened the door we both heaved a sigh of relief; I, because *she* was not a saggy-titted old woman with poorly dyed red hair; and she because *I* did not appear at the door with a butcher knife and "I'm the Antichrist" tattooed on my forehead.

She took me to her home, a place I can only describe as a magical gingerbread house, surrounded by beautiful gardens. The rooms were full of art and books and comfortable furniture. I was so very relieved. She was wonderful, knowledgeable, and wise. I bombarded her with questions that she answered candidly.

Our conversation naturally turned to the subject of *Liber AL vel Legis, The Book of the Law*. A year or so earlier I had followed the instructions (or at least I thought I was doing so) laid out in the Class A Comment on the text. I destroyed my first copy of the book after the first reading. I asked her, "Why did I have to destroy my copy of *The Book of the Law* after first reading it?"

Her answer was this. "You've got an obedience streak in you dear. You're going to have to watch that."

I had found my teacher.

Phyllis Seckler would be my formal A∴A∴ contact, and also my dear Sister in the O.T.O. which was led at the time be her then-husband Grady Louis McMurtry (Caliph Hymenaeus Alpha, 777). I would take my first two O.T.O. initiations, my Minerval and First Degree, in their home in Dublin. Shortly after my first degree initiation I wrote a little poem called *Water Closet—Caliph's Advice*, which I wrote to immortalize his answer to my question, "What advice can you give to a young magician first starting out on the path?"

He answered with a cavalier lilt to his voice, "I asked Crowley the same thing the first time I met him. He simply said, 'Try to visit the water closet whenever you can. You never know when you'll get the chance again.'

Phyllis was kind enough to publish in an issue of her marvelous magazine, *In The Continuum*. I'm afraid it might not make too much sense to those unfamiliar with the Man of Earth degrees of the O.T.O. but for those who are I hope very much that you enjoy.

Love is the law, love under will.

Water Closet (Caliph's Advice)
Lon Milo DuQuette (August 1976)

Adepts and Mahatmas

Dance widdershins

While they Devil, and Beast, and Oz it.

An aspirant's day mysteriously begins

With a visit to the water closet.

Forefinger on left nostril

Thumb on its mate.

He blows out his air and he draws it.

With post nasal drip, pranayama is great,

While sitting in the water closet.

In Mass 44

Enflaméd he prays

So deep that he had to gauze it.

A comfort to know

Repairs can be made

By a visit to the water closet.

Hanged Man, Noah's Ark, Osiris and Seth

Effect and all things which cause it.

How much like birth, How very much like
death

Is a visit to the water closet,

Grimoire of Thelema

FOREWORD FOR THE 2011 EDITION[1]

Do what thou wilt shall be the whole of the Law.

Magick is a lonely art. It must ever be so, because ultimately we are each a universe unto our self. The 'whatever-it-is-we-are' was alone when it incarnated into this corporeal dimension; and it will be alone at the timeless instant we shuffle off this mortal coil. But as we labor through the measured ticks of space-time on *this* side of the pylons of birth and death our 'whatever-it-is-we-are' is surrounded and assailed by a vast assortment of other 'whatever-it-is-we-ares'—other monads of consciousness who are also universes unto themselves—and some of these other universes are fellow magicians.

Magick is also (first and foremost) a self-transformational art. It may be the magician's intent to effect changes in his or her outer life circumstances, *i.e.,* "I want the girl next door to fall in love with me . . ." but the success of any magical operation designed to bring about that romantic outcome will most assuredly be in large part the consequences of the *magician becoming transformed* into the type of person the girl next door falls in love with.

I'm sure there are knowledgeable and skilled magicians who will disagree with my sweeping assertion that *the only thing I can change with Magick is myself.* It is of

---

1   Written for Rodney Orpheus, *Grimoire of Thelema,* Stockholm: Abrahadabra Press, 2011.

course a statement that is impossible for me to prove or disprove, and frankly I'm not inclined or motivated to try. I'm not trying to establish or defend magical doctrine. I simply know that for me—at this season of my life—at this moment in my magical career—the thing that needs to change the most in my world is *me*.

I have to confess, the prospect of magick being a form of consciously directed self-evolution was not what initially attracted to me to the art so many years ago. Naturally, I told myself that I was doing all this to gain enlightenment—to achieve spiritual liberation, but in truth it was the allure of wearing a black-hooded robe and strutting around in darkened temples brandishing my wand and sword against terrible demons cowering in terrified obedience before my radiant adeptship.

Man! Would I look *cool* doing that!

No matter how noble and altruistic my conscious pretenses were, Lon Milo DuQuette (the post-adolescent magician) inwardly desired power—power to master the cruel and chaotic circumstances of my life—power to right the wrongs I was witnessing in the world around me—power to set things straight and in harmony with my own (obviously *already enlightened*) vision of personal, moral, social, political, and spiritual absolutes.

As comically deluded as I might have been, there is of course nothing fundamentally wrong with such youthful and militant idealism—nothing wrong with wanting to change the world for the better and setting to work to do just that. I guess the biggest flaw in my aspirational game-plan was that I was overlooking the fact that in order for me to use magick to begin making these changes I would first have to consciously evolve into a real magician. As luck would have it, I would early in my career come under the influence and tutelage of magicians who would each in their unique way (either by positive example, negative example, or admonition) make sure I never forgot this fundamental fact of life.

Foremost among my senior mentors were Phyllis Secker (Soror Meral), Grady L. McMurtry (Hymenaeus Alpha, 777), Helen Parsons-Smith (Soror Grimaud), and Francis (Israel) Regardie. All of these dear people are now deceased.

McMurtry and Regardie trained directly under Aleister Crowley, and Seckler had been the student of Jane Wolfe, a student of Crowley's and a one-time resident of Crowley's famous *Abbey of Thelema* in Sicily. Parsons-Smith was the double widow of Jack Parsons (the famed magician and rocket scientist) and Wilfred P. Smith—both were, at different times, Masters of Agape Lodge, O.T.O. in Southern California.

These colorful people kept me from being entirely alone in the early years of my quest. Because of their efforts (and more often *despite* their efforts) I was in the mid 1970s baptized in the magick fire of Thelema. With their encouragement, cynicism, and guidance, I formally took up the disciplines of Crowley's magical orders, the A∴A∴ and Ordo Templi Orients.

My A∴A∴ work began under the guidance of Seckler and was (or should have been) an entirely private affair. My O.T.O. experience, on the other hand, required me to work in a more public manner and with other magicians all over the world—sometimes many other magicians. In fact, an important aspect of the O.T.O.'s magical curriculum is the development of the individual magician's ability to work in concert (and *survive*) within the complexities of a uniquely organized society populated by cast of militantly independent magicians (some of whom are as intractable, imperfect and flawed as myself!). It's a very important part of the magical training of an O.T.O. initiate.

As you might expect, Crowley didn't make the O.T.O. ordeal an easy one. In fact, I've known more promising magicians to wreck on the shoals of the Order's societal challenges than for any other reason. More often than not, however, I usually come to see the wisdom and genius of Crowley's magical vetting process.

Whether or not they have established a formal A∴A∴ relationship, a great many O.T.O. initiates and others who consider themselves Thelemic magicians embark on the study and practice of the various rituals Crowley developed for the edification of A∴A∴ magicians. The systematic practice of these rituals *vis a vis* the magician's personal initiatory climb up the *Tree of Life* of consciousness is generally viewed in Thelemic circles as "doing the work."

The work is certainly there to do. The rituals and a few commentaries are published in a plethora of sources. One of the finest collections is found in the magnificently ponderous *Liber ABA, Book IV* [2], but for many years most of us relied almost exclusively on those ritual "Libers" that appeared in the Appendices of *Magick in Theory and Practice*. [3]

Armed with little more than these Libers and the roadmap of the *Tree of Life*, four generations of magicians have set out alone on the Thelemic path of return; dissecting, cross-referencing, and trying to make sense of

---

2 Aleister Crowley with Mary Desti and Leila Waddell. *Magick—Liber ABA—Book IV*, York Beach, Maine: Weiser Books, Inc., second revised edition, 1997.
3 Aleister Crowley- *Magick in Theory and Practice*, Paris: Lecram Press 1929. Reprint, New York: Magickal Childe Publications, 1990.

the bewildering subtleties of Crowley's evolving thought, and then attempting to transfer that understanding to the temple environment in coherent ceremonies that can be performed by (and for the benefit of) one person. To say it is a challenge to the lone magician would be a beastly understatement.

Yes. Magick is a lonely art. But does it always need to be *that* lonely? I don't believe so—and neither does my Brother Rodney Orpheus. People—even magicians—sometimes need other people. There are moments in my life when I don't know *what* I am, *where* I am, or *who* I am unless I can see myself momentarily reflected in the souls of others around me.

The term "Thelemic group ritual" may sound like an oxymoron, but it needn't *be* one. As Brother Orpheus reveals, many of Crowley's most significant rituals started out as group operations. For me, it is profoundly helpful (at times even necessary) to see the complex dynamics of my own inner magical mechanisms portrayed as different "officers" in a ritual. I can, and of course *must* eventually integrate all these officers into myself, but first I have to know who they are, what they do, and what they mean to me. That is most easily and elegantly done by seeing them operate in a group drama.

I took one look at Rodney's group treatments of the *Ritual of the Mark of the Beast* and the *Invocation of Horus* and was thrown back in my chair in stunned admiration, "My gods! Why hasn't someone done this before?" This might sound like a rhetorical question, but in fact it does indeed have an answer. The reason someone hasn't done this before is because there are presently very few individuals living today who are qualified by education and experience to do so, and even fewer with the writing talent and communication skills to bring it all to life on the printed page. Brother Orpheus is the incarnation of both these aspects of genius. Whether he is expanding upon classic Crowley rituals or creating and developing his own Thelemic ceremonies, the magician reader can be confident he or she is in good hands.

Magick may be a lonely art, but that doesn't mean we must always be alone on our journey—and it doesn't mean we won't always need friends.

Love is the law, love under will.

Abrahadabra

Understanding Aleister Crowley's Thelemic Magic

"Do what thou wilt shall be the whole of the Law."

First let me say that this is the second version of this Foreword that I've written for this new edition of *Abrahadabra*. After reading my first attempt the author (speaking with the voice of candor reserved exclusively for the best of friends and the bitterest of enemies) lamented that it was "a potted bio" of Aleister Crowley that missed the mark entirely. While I remain firm in my belief that it was a damned good "potted bio" I must confess I see the wisdom of his criticisms.

"*Abrahadabra* is not about Aleister Crowley and should not be colored by his history, reputation, or personality. *Abrahadabra* is about the *practice* of the magick of Thelema—a system of physical, mental, and spiritual training and discipline based on two fundamental principals: *Do what thou wilt shall be the whole of the Law. Love is the law, love under will.*"

By writing this book, the author reveals (whether he cares to admit it or not) his profound understanding

---

1 Written for Rodney Orpheus, *Abrahadabra: Understanding Aleister Crowley's Thelemic Magic,* Newburyport, Massachusetts: Weiser Books, 2005. First published by Looking Glass Press, Stockholm, 1995.

of the *"Do"* in Do what thou wilt . . . " and challenges and inspires the reader to share his commitment to action rather than argument, deeds rather than platitudes, experience rather than theories.

He succeeds mightily at this. He fails, however, at keeping his own personality out of the text—and for this the reader should be deeply grateful. His casual and humorous style serves to lower the blood pressure and causes one to immediately identify on a personal level with his thoughts, attitudes, and conclusions.

It takes a particular (some say peculiar) kind of individual to write unpretentiously and unhypocritically about the practical aspects of Thelemic magick. Rodney Orpheus, unlike many practicing (and published) occultists, has a life. He is a rock-star, a recording-artist, a business-executive, and high-degree initiate-officer of one of the most revered and influential magical societies in the world. His life, however, does not revolve around any of these hyphenated Rodneys. In true Thelemic style, they each revolve around *him*. So it should be for all who tread the way of Thelema, a path where the individual and the individual's true Will is the focus of the Great Work.

But, where does one start the "work" of the Great Work? Without some kind of beginner's guide the study and practice of Thelemic Magick is like trying to learn to swim by jumping into the deep end of the pool and doing whatever you have to do to keep from drowning. Many have done just that, and (having survived the ordeal and human nature being what it is) carry the machismo attitude of, "I did it the hard way, so should everybody else." This attitude is, to quote Al

Franken's New Age counselor, Stuart Smalley, is just *stinkin' thinkin'*.

There will always be ordeals, (with or without helpful manuals such as this) and no one can presume to judge the circumstances of another's magical life. Mr. Orpheus had the benefit of life in Holy Orders and the mentorship of initiate instructors. Even with these enviable advantages, I'm sure he will be the first to admit that his early studies and practices were plagued unnecessarily with time-consuming confusion as to how best to proceed.

Abrahadabra—A Beginner's Guide to Thelemic Magick[2], is a precious gift to all who wish to immediately embark upon the fundamental practices and meditations of Thelemic Magick and assure themselves that their magical careers are being built on a firm and balanced foundation. I am delighted to see it appear in this new edition.

Love is the law, love under will.

---

2   Subsequently sub-titled: *Understanding Aleister Crowley's Thelemic Magic.*

Thelema

An Introduction to the Life, Work, and Philosophy of Aleister Crowley

INTRODUCTION TO THE 2018 EDITION[1]

Then saith the prophet and slave of the beauteous one: Who am I, and what shall be the sign? So she answered him, bending down, a lambent flame of blue, all-touching, all penetrant, her lovely hands upon the black earth, & her lithe body arched for love, and her soft feet not hurting the little flowers: Thou knowest! And the sign shall be my ecstasy, the consciousness of the continuity of existence, the omnipresence of my body.

LIBER AL VEL LEGIS, I. v. 26.

Do what thou wilt shall be the whole of the Law.

Aleister Crowley died in 1947 at the age of seventy-two. The whereabouts of his ashes remain a mystery. For twenty years after his death, his name and his voluminous writings remained for the most part undiscovered, unread, and unappreciated by all but a tiny band of

---

1 Written for Collin D. Campbell, *Thelema: An Introduction to the Life, Work, and Philosophy of Aleister Crowley*, Woodbury, Minnesota: Llewellyn Publications, 2018.

former disciples, bohemian artists, and a handful of revolutionary thinkers. Then, on June 1, 1967 Crowley's unmistakable visage appeared (glaring out at us from between the faces of Indian holy man, Swami Sri Yukteswar, and sex-goddess, Mae West) on the (then) most eagerly-awaited *objet d'art* on the planet—the album cover of the Beatles newest LP, *Sgt. Pepper's Lonely Hearts Club Band*.

The cover art was the creation of artist Peter Blake, who wanted to surround the band with what he called "a magical crowd." The inclusion of Swami Yukteswar, Paramahansa Yogananda, and other Hindu yogis was George Harrison's idea. Among characters John Lennon "liked" was the poet and "wickedest man in the world," Aleister Crowley.

Do not misunderstand me. I'm not suggesting that the Beatles or Peter Blake were directly responsible for the spiritual and cultural upheavals of the 1960s, or the storms that are still echoing (actively or reactively) in today's chaotic world. Nor am I suggesting John Lennon or Peter Blake should be singled out and credited for igniting the revival of interest and appreciation of Aleister Crowley, Thelema, magick, or any of the progressive spiritual movements that continue to proliferate today. Like all great artists, at pivotal moments in history, these sensitive pioneers were merely among the first to react and respond to the effects of a dramatic shift in human consciousness.

Consciously or subconsciously their works gave voice to the new reality. The art they and their contemporaries created during those golden years pealed like a mighty bell that vibrated with the master "note" of this new universal consciousness. A note that rang out like a broadcast signal that triggered sympathetic responses in the hearts and souls of all who were poised and ripe for awakening.

The concept of evolving shifts in consciousness is not a new one. Almost every ancient culture had it version of "ages" (*i.e.,* golden age when humanity *walked with the gods,* or dark age when the *gods abandon us).* The Hindus call the various ages "Yugas"[2] which predictively rise and fall in cycles of thousands of millennia as our entire solar system careens around the galactic center in a huge elliptical orbit.

Astrologers have their own version of the cosmic cycles based on the apparent backward movement of the signs of the zodiac relative to the position of the rising sun on the spring equinox. It takes 2,160 years to traverse one complete sign, and most astrologers compute that we have recently passed (or will soon pass) from the astrological *Age of Pisces* into the *Age of Aquarius.*

Now, you may think it odd that I should begin these introductory words to Mr. Campbell's marvelous book about *Thelema* by talking about 1960s pop stars and Hindu theories of astrology, but (in *my* mind at least) it illustrates the most important, thing to first understand when attempting to comprehend the meaning and significance of Thelema; that is, whether any of us are consciously aware of it or not, within the last hundred years or so there has been a profound and dramatic shift (advance; transformation; mutation; amendment; metamorphosis; transfiguration; leap; refocus) in human consciousness. We are all now functioning in an entirely new and different reality than the one in which our recent

---

2 I can't resist pointing out an amazing coincidence. One of the most respected Hindu experts on Yugas was Swami Sri Yukteswar, the man standing beside Aleister Crowley on the cover of Sgt. Pepper's Lonely Hearts Club Band.

ancestors functioned. The old ways of doing business on every level of our lives will never again work exactly like they used to.

It's not just the fact that our tastes have changed; or that we hear music or appreciate art differently; it's not just the fact that our understanding of mathematics has exploded *inwardly* to irrational quantum levels, or that our understanding of astronomy has exploded *outwardly* and erased all old time and dimensional limitations; it's not just the fact many of the most fortunate among us have the collected the store of ten thousand years of human knowledge at our electronic fingertips, or that many of us are now routinely accustomed to educational, social and economic liberties. No. All these things are simply symptoms and by-products, of a new essential *factor* in the great formula of human consciousness. The new factor isn't anything complex or particularly esoteric. It is, however, significant enough to cause a new mutation in the DNA of our consciousness. The new factor is simply:

A new level of self-awareness.

This might not sound very sexy or dramatic, but, in this *new* reality, *nothing* could be *more* sexy or dramatic. This new awakening is disarmingly simple and fundamental. But, like the invisible wind, its existence only makes itself known by the effects it has on other things. It's really hard to make observations about self-awareness because the observer is the object being observed. Actually, the whole thing is simpler than it sounds. Allow me to offer an illustration of shifts in self-awareness.

Our very ancient ancestors, while being cognizant of day and night, darkness and light, heat and cold, comfort and discomfort, were primarily focused on day-to-day, moment-to-moment issues of immediate self-preservation. All human activities, whether, conscious or instinctual, revolved around the preservation of the body through protection, nourishment, and the biological perpetuation of the species. All other observations or speculations about life or the world around us were projected against the screen of this reality and interpreted to satisfy these immediate needs. Everything about our ancestors conscious and subconscious lives (religious concepts and expressions, gods, spirits, myths, rituals, even art) was interpreted by the self-identity of a creature competing with other creatures for food and survival.

The metaphoric "Gods" that visibly ruled this level of consciousness-reality was the Earth itself, and the Earth's human equivalent, Woman, in particular, the Mother. Crowley named this phase of evolutionary consciousness the *Aeon of Isis*, after the great Egyptian Mother Goddess.

Eventually, as our understanding of the world around us increased a bit, our self-awareness shifted and received a fine-tuning. We started to see ourselves as existing in a more complex and wondrous environment that we could partially manage and control. No longer did we see ourselves only as just another competing creature, but as a master creature that could exploit other creatures and our environment. If we were cold, we could build or even travel to warmer lands. If we were hungry, we could cultivate plants rather than forage for them. We could domesticate and breed beasts rather than hunt them. Our eyes turned to the sky and it became evident that the sun made the plants grow, and lured animals to come eat the plants. Summer and winter were sun-triggered events that needed to be dealt with. Gods and religions evolved to accommodate the new reality—the new self-identity. Existence was now seen as a partnership of sun and earth, father and mother.

But, along with this wakening came the new mystery formula—the formula of a Sun which dies every day, and almost dies every winter. And this new formula brought with it our terrible preoccupation with death. Plants die and the dead seeds are buried and then magically reborn; the Sun dies and needs to be magically resurrected; it only follows that *I* die and *I* will need to be magically brought back to life.

Crowley named this phase of evolutionary consciousness the *Aeon of Osiris*, after the great Egyptian God of Death and Resurrection. It is a formula based on our self-identity with the Sun that dies and is magically reborn. It is the level of consciousness that has fashioned the reality of our most recent ancestors—their religion, politics, war, culture, art, literature, and civilization itself—everything.

All that has changed. While the decaying, zombie remnants of the Aeon of Osiris will likely haunt us for the foreseeable future, a new Age has dawned. Crowley named this new phase of evolutionary consciousness the *Aeon of Horus*, the child of Isis and Osiris. Instead of our conscious reality arising from the need for nourishment (as in the Aeon of Isis), or our obsession with overcoming death (as in the Aeon of Osiris) we now simple *grow*—as naturally, as innocently, and as joyously as a child—a child who will accept no limits to its potential growth.

As unbelievably simple as it sounds, the factor that characterizes the essence of our new self-identity . . . the factor that characterizes our new level of consciousness, is our universally accepted observation that the *sun does not die*. It shines eternally. This simple new reality has permanently upgraded the operating system of human consciousness. The sun does not die. We do not die. The sun shines eternally—we shine eternally. We now function as a unit of self-awareness that deep down inside knows it *does not die*—that knows there is no off-switch—that knows we've always been *on* and we'll always be *on*.

In the Aeon of Horus eternal life is now simply understood as, "the consciousness of the continuity of existence."

Like Lao Tzu's mysterious Tao, Thelema defies objective definition.

Is it a Philosophy? Although there are philosophic nuances to Thelema, it is bigger than philosophy. But, if we were to attempt to explain Thelema to someone who needs to approach things from a philosophic angle we could say, Thelema is a "Rational philosophy of spiritual self-sufficiency."

Is it a religion? Although there are infinite ways to incorporate your understanding of Thelema in religious forms of expression, Thelema is bigger than religion. But, if we were to attempt to explain Thelema to someone that needs to approach things from a classic religious angle we could say, "Thelema is a rational religion of Sun worship ... if you define the word "Sun" as also meaning *yourself.*

Is it a Magical system? Although many Magicians consider themselves Thelemites, Thelema is bigger than any particular, system, technique or study. Indeed, once one has comfortably adjusted to the new level of self-awareness Thelema serves only to enhance, energize and hybridize whatever philosophical, religious, or magical systems or schools of thought you hold dear.

Is it Crowley's magical societies, O.T.O. and A∴A∴? Although these two organizations propagate the "Law of Thelema" and the teachings of Aleister, Thelema is bigger that any organization, order, or school of instruction. As a matter of fact, Thelema is bigger than the Book of the Law, or Aleister Crowley, or anything in heaven or earth . . . but *you*.

Love is the law, love under will.

After the Angel

An Account of the Abramelin Operation

A Six-Month Working to Attain the Knowledge and Conversation of the Holy Guardian Angel

PREFACE TO THE 2011 EDITION[1]

Knowledge and Conversation of the Holy Guardian Angel is the primary goal of the ceremonial magician and must be achieved before any other meaningful magical acts can be accomplished.

The Holy Guardian Angel (the Secret Lover) will be the magician's teacher, lover, mentor and guide through the higher levels of initiation.

Whether one considers oneself a ceremonial magician or not, the fact remains that the above experience, no matter what it is called, is a prerequisite for complete spiritual liberation.[2]

---

1 Written for Marcus Katz, *After the Angel, An Account of the Abramelin Operation,* New York: Forge Press, 2011.

2 DuQuette, Lon Milo, and Hyatt, Christopher S. *Sex Magic, Tantra & Tarot: The Way of the Secret Lover,* Las Vegas, Nevada: New Falcon Publications, 1991; 3rd, revised and expanded edition, 2008, p. 13.

On July 11th, 1969, I celebrated my 21st birthday by getting deliciously high on Afghan hashish with my friend and songwriting partner, Charley D. Harris.[3] The occasion was doubly celebratory because we had just inked a new recording contract with Epic Records and were preparing material for a second single and an album for that prestigious label—a work we were sure would finally bring us the fame and fortune we believed we so richly deserved.

Charley and I weren't just wannabe rock stars; at least not in our own minds. No. We fancied ourselves troubadours of cosmic consciousness, magical bards, mystic musicians, psychedelic hippy poets surfing the tsunami of cultural consciousness created by the patron saints of our generation—Bob Dylan, Dr. Timothy Leary, and the Beatles. Even our silly love songs were written as thinly-veiled hymns to transcendent deity. At that sweet, green moment of life our youth acknowledged no limits to our magick; and knowing no limits, there *were* none.

With oddly egoless bravado we resolved to write a new song on the spot. I leaned across my beloved Gibson B-45 12 string and plucked an "Occult Dictionary" from the bookcase, closed my eyes, opened it at random and blindly pinned my finger to a page. It rested on the words, "Inner Man." Three bowls of hash later we had our song:

Deep within you,
Softly hear me sing;
Find me if you will.
I've never not been anything,
And I always will.

---

3   Charles Dennis Harris, 1941-2016, (a.k.a., Charley Packard).

All in the All and the All in All.
(I am the Inner Man.)
All in the All and the All in All.
(I am the Inner Man.)

See how each night becomes the day,
Born with each new dawn.
Death cannot claim the Inner Man,
That's how life goes on.

All in the All and the All in All.
(I am the Inner Man.)
All in the All and the All in All.
(I am the Inner Man.)

And when you find the Inner Man,
With your journey through,
Smiling, you find the one to tell,
It was always you.

All in the All and the All in All.
(I am the Inner Man.)
All in the All and the All in All.
(I am the Inner Man.)[4]

---

4   *Inner Man.* From the album, *Charley D & Milo,* (Epic Records, 1970). Lyrics
    and music by Lon Milo DuQuette and Charles D. Harris, BMI, 1970.

Our lyrics didn't spring from the depths of any character-building life experiences or profound mystical traumas. Those terrible adventures still awaited us in the future. But I believe we were nonetheless on to something very real—something very important (other than that excellent hashish).

Our song was a corny cliché; naïve and pretentious. But to tell the truth, reading these lyrics 42 years later I am still impressed by the message. In fact, I'm hard-pressed to think of a more concise summation of the ineffable spiritual experience (event-phenomenon-illumination) that is the subject of Mr. Katz's remarkable book.

Knowledge and Conversation of the Holy Guardian Angel (K & C of the HGA) is a rather silly sounding expression for a very serious spiritual event. One is almost embarrassed to say the words when discussing the matter with people unfamiliar with the esoteric history of *The Book of The Sacred Magic of Abramelin the Mage as Delivered by Abraham the Jew Unto His Son Lamech—A Grimoire of The Fifteenth Century*,[5] or the Golden Dawn, or the works of Aleister Crowley. It is not exactly the same "Guardian Angel" to whom little Catholic children address their bedtime prayers . . . or is it?

The intense and heroic magical operation that Mr. Katz performed and that he so ably describes in his book was created by the magician, Abraham of Worms (c.1362—1558), to trigger a tangible and objective mystical experience—an eyes-wide-open moment of ecstatic union even more real, life-altering and memorable than one's first romantically charged adolescent kiss. It is the ultimate *consummation devoutly to be wish'd*.

---

5 Abraham of Worms. *The Book of the Sacred Magic of Abramelin the Mage*, trans. S.L. Macgregor Mathers, New York: Dover, 1975.

According to Abraham's theory we are each in a sense an *unfinished* human being (a slumbering princess) until we have been *kissed* by (united with) our questing prince (the HGA). The HGA, on the other hand, remains an unfinished spiritual being (a prince who will never be a king until he has married a princess).

Of course, the entire cast of characters in this fairy-tale are simply metaphors for levels of consciousness and the mechanics of our evolving *identity with* those levels of consciousness. But sleeping princesses and hunky princes and kings and queens and awaking kisses and weddings and babies are *pretty damned good* metaphors for this process; because the key that holds it all together ... indeed, the key to the nature of consciousness itself, from iron and rocks, to light, energy and godhead itself, is *Love*.

But is love, as the Beatles sang, really "All you need?" In my book, *Ask Baba Lon: Answers to Questions of Life and Magick*,[6] I try to answer the question, "What is the fastest way to unite with the HGA?"

> Knowledge and Conversation of the Holy Guardian Angel is a love thing. Work on developing the ability to fall hopelessly, blissfully, passionately in love with GOD (or whatever your object of supreme divinity is). Each of us is already trying to mate with our HGA every time we fall in love with someone or something. It's not really the person or object of our devotion we're falling in love with, we're falling in love with a perfected ideal (something that

---

6   DuQuette, Lon Milo. *Ask Baba Lon: Answers to Questions of Life and Magick.* Las Vegas: New Falcon Publications, 2011.

no person or thing could in reality ever live up to). That ideal is the Angel. That perfected ideal is really us (a fact we'll discover when we and the Angel are united).

Until then, we're already well armed with the only tool we need to lure the Angel to us: intense, insane, romantic naiveté; a devotion so consuming it would embarrass us to death if we weren't so blinded by Love . . .[7]

The Abramelin operation is designed to systematically build up the magician's devotional muscles in a relatively safe and balanced manner; a process that (for those of us in the west) is not always easy to give ourselves over to. In fact, the operation seems ingeniously designed to gradually trick the rational mind into surrendering its sovereignty . . . at least long enough to become irrationally open to the influx of divine consciousness. What is especially valuable about the way Mr. Katz has applied the Abramelin operation to his own life, is the way he performed this "magical retirement" amid the distractions and the madding crowd of his everyday/work-a-day world. I believe he succeeded in striking this delicate balance that is so necessary if one desires to ascend to heavenly levels of consciousness while not prematurely abandoning one's incarnational responsibilities, and opportunities.

It is fair for the magician to ask, "What incarnational duty could possibly more important than Knowledge and Conversation of the Holy Guardian Angel? Why do I need to strike a balance in between the world of

---

7 *Ibid.* 126.

karmic entanglements and the of world of enlightenment? Why shouldn't I simply abandon everything in my life and pursue with one-pointed ardor this spiritual illumination?" In *Ask Baba Lon* I try to address this question as well.

> ... Knowledge and Conversation of the Holy Guardian Angel is a level of consciousness, and the straightest path to the HGH is devotion. If you can fall completely and helplessly in love with God you are there. If this means you find yourself in a loincloth jumping up and down on a street corner blissfully singing Hare Krishna (or Hare Crowley), then so be it. It won't matter to you, because you and the beloved will be joined in ecstatic union.
>
> If, however, you feel in your heart-of-hearts (and that's where the Holy Guardian Angel lives) that you still have some mission to accomplish in this incarnation before hopping on the train and taking the "straightest path" to bliss land, then you should start shopping around to see what your mission is and customize your devotional quest for the Angel in order to harmonize and manifest your life's mission (Will).[8]

And what about me? Has Lon Milo DuQuette achieved Knowledge and Conversation of the Holy Guardian Angel?

---

8 *Ibid.* p.123.

That also is a fair question to ask. If I have, I confess it didn't occur as I pictured it would the first time I read *The Sacred Magic of Abramelin the Mage*. If I have achieved K & C of the HGA, it came as a realization not of something that happened to me, but a realization of what I now am. Awake . . . or at least more awake than the boy who wrote "I am the Inner Man."

Perhaps the name of my Holy Guardian Angel is "Baba Lon" or Rabbi Lamed Ben Clifford. Perhaps that's the way it always works. Together you and the angel become somebody else . . . someone who writes love notes to oneself.

PART FIVE

ENOCHIAN MAGICK

~~~~~~~~~~~~~~~~~~~~~~~~~~~~~~~~~

Teach me (O creator of all things), to have correct knowledge and understanding, for your wisdom is all that I desire. Speak your word in my ear (O creator of all things) and set your wisdom in my heart.

—John Dee

The Complete Enochian Dictionary

FOREWORD FOR THE 2001 EDITION[1]

His life is a watch or a vision

Between a sleep and a sleep.

ALGERNON SWINBURNE

ATALANTA IN CALYDON

An eternal debate rages between those who believe in the objective existence of spiritual entities, and those who believe that all such phenomena, no matter how apparently substantial, are entirely subjective experiences. Perhaps both schools of thought are correct. Where angels, demons, and spirits are concerned, I personally believe *it's all in your head—you just have no idea how big your head is.* Or, to quote my pseudepigraphic guru, Rabbi Lamed Ben Clifford, "Yes the spirits are real. Yes the spirits are imaginary. Most of us, however, cannot imagine how real our imaginations are."

I can, with no small measure of confidence, generally defend this position with jabs of well-worn qabalistic suppositions concerning the nature of consciousness and the functions of the various parts of the soul, and the

---

1   Written for Donald C. Laycock, *The Complete Enochian Dictionary*, Newburyport, Massachusetts: Weiser Books, 2001.

left hook of Carl Jung. There have been times, however, when my field theory has been mightily challenged. Mr. Laycock's *Complete Enochian Dictionary* played a curious role in one such magical bout.

In 1978, as part of my perceived duties as an O.T.O.[2] lodge-master, I began what would become a twenty-three-year weekly magick class at my home in Costa Mesa, California. At the time, I was hard-pressed to stay one jump ahead of the enthusiastic aspirants who crowded my living-room floor each Thursday evening, and within a year or so I realized that if I intended to continue teaching, I was eventually going to have learn more myself.

My magick library was pitifully small in those days. My newest treasure was a first edition of *Gems from the Equinox*[3] that contained a selection of books, articles, essays, and rituals from Aleister Crowley's monumental work, *The Equinox*.[4] I combed through it to see if I could find something novel and exotic to occupy our Thursday nights for a while. I settled on *Liber LXXXIV, vel Chanokh—A Brief Abstract of the Symbolic Representation of the Universe Derived by Dr. John Dee Through the Skrying of Sir Edward Kelly*. It is Crowley's introduction to the complex and beautiful magical art form that has come to be known as *Enochian*. I didn't know it at the time, but *Chanokh* (and the book you are now holding in your hands) would dramatically change the course of my life.

---

2 Ordo Templi Orientis.
3 *Gems From the Equinox, Instructions by Aleister Crowley for His Own Magical Order.* Ed. Israel Regardie. Most recent edition Scottsdale, Arizona: New Falcon Publications, 1992.
4 *The Equinox Volume 1, Numbers 1-10.* Aleister Crowley, et al. Most recent edition York Beach, Maine: Samuel Weiser, Inc., 1998.

At first I found *Chanokh* completely unfathomable. I read it, re-read it and checked it against the Enochian material in Regardie's *Golden Dawn*.[5] After a day or two of whimpering, things finally started to make a little sense. The material that treated upon the evocation of angels of the four Elemental Tablets appeared to be the logical place to start the class.

Each Elemental Tablet is made up of 156 lettered squares, each of which is divided so to represent a truncated pyramid. Each has its own particular mixture of elements determined by a most impressive application of Hermetic logic. An angel (whose name is the letter of the square) "lives" in every one of the pyramids. These single-letter-named angels are modular and join with their neighbors to form bigger angels with longer names and more complex attributes and duties. It is truly an elegant system.

My plan was to keep the class occupied for a few weeks drawing and coloring their own tablets while I consulted with Dr. Regardie and constructed a set of three-dimensional tablets. Regardie was not keen on the idea. He told me that to his knowledge no one had ever done such a thing before, and that the Enochian angels were dangerous enough when they inhabited flat tablets. He cautioned, "Don't give them dimensional elbow-room." I joked, and suggested that *his* angels were probably in a bad mood because they were all squished up inside his flat tablets. I went ahead and prevailed upon a lodge brother to cut 624 wooden truncated pyramids. These I would eventually prepare, paint, and assemble into the Four Elemental Tablets (one each for Fire, Water, Air, & Earth.)

---

5   The Golden Dawn. Ed, Israel Regardie. Most recent edition St. Paul: Llewellyn
    Publications, 1992.

The night of our first evocation arrived. I prepared our living-room temple for the evocation of Laidrom, the Mars Senior of the Tablet of Earth[6]. The temple opening and operating procedures are outlined admirably in *Chanokh* so there was very little to do but follow directions. I smugly congratulated myself on being so well prepared. What I wasn't prepared for, however, was the possibility that the evocation might actually work.

The first student to arrive was D. R., who proudly handed me his newly acquired first edition of Laycock's *The Complete Enochian Dictionary*[7]—the first one I had ever seen. As I always do when someone hands me something rare or expensive, I feigned profound gratitude and gushed, "Oh! Thank you." He quickly snatched it back out of my hands.

Once the rest of the class arrived I asked for a volunteer to read the Call in the angelic language and sit in the visionary driver's seat. To my great anxiety our only volunteer was David Wilson, the most cynical member of the class. I was certain that our class curmudgeon would receive no vision whatsoever and all of our efforts would be the target of his ridicule for many months to come. Still, he was willing to give it a try so I switched on our little tape recorder and we proceeded.

After I banished and opened the temple, David read the Call twice, closed his eyes and sat quietly for only a few seconds. Then, to all of our surprise, he casually started to describe in great detail his vision of a desert

---

6   Each Elemental Tablet has a Solar King and six Planetary Seniors. These seven spirits are very high on the Enochian hierarchical ladder.

7   The Complete Enochian Dictionary—A Dictionary of the Angelic Language as Revealed to Dr. John Dee and Edward Kelley. by Donald C. Laycock. First edition London. Askin Publishers, LTD, 1978. Subsequent editions York Beach, Maine: Weiser Books, Inc., 1994 & 2001.

of white crystalline sand that sprouted columns of volcanic rock.

We were all thrilled. I asked if he saw any living things, an angel or a spirit. He said "No." I encouraged him to repeat the Call a third time. As soon as he was finished he excitedly described an enormous black cone arising from beneath the sand. David fell silent for a moment. He told us the cone was opening. Then, with a shout that startled us all . . . "It's him! It's him! I see him."

He described a large humanoid figure seemingly constructed from the same material as the cone. It had no face, its head was egg-shaped and flat in front. Its fingerless hands had the appearance of mittens. "This is Laidrom!" David announced reverently.

We were all in shock. None of us were prepared for this. David reached for a pad of paper and a pencil and scribbled down a few notes and a sketch. Before I could stutter out words of welcome, David let out a nervous giggle and said, "Lon, I feel like . . . I feel . . . I could make strange sounds."

"Go with it!" I don't think I really meant it.

"Naw-n tahelo hoh athayzo raygayef . . . this is . . ."

"No! Relax, let it happen!" I tried to sound calm.

"I mean it, I feel like and idiot. I'm too . . . *sil-si anxilxi-to-da-arp nan-ta* (inaudible) . . . *ef* . . . *efe thar-zi*. I'm sorry . . . that's all. Nothing like this has ever happened before. I just felt like doing it."

I didn't know what to say. I finally salvaged the presence of mind to thank Laidrom for appearing. I was painfully embarrassed that I couldn't think of anything to say to this perfectly well-mannered angel standing in my living-room. I finally stuttered something stupid to the effect that we really appreciated him stopping by, and we'd sure like to visit with him again sometime soon, then I hurriedly closed and banished the temple.

For a few seconds, no one said a word. Then everyone started talking at once. I rewound the tape and we listened to the strange words that had tumbled out of David's mouth. Of course, they didn't make any sense, but it was such a thrill to hear them.

We rewound the tape repeatedly and eventually transcribed three audible strings of syllables:

naw-n tahelo hoh athayzo raygayeff

zil-zi-anzilzi-lo-da-arp nan-ta (inaudible)

ef . . . efee thar-zi.

We referred to D. R.'s *The Complete Enochian Dictionary* and in short order discovered,

Nanta, elo Hoath zorge ef.

"Spirit of Earth, first worshiper friendly visit."

Zil zien

"stretch forth hands"

Zilodarp Nanta

"stretch forth and conquer Spirit of Earth"

Ef etharzi

"visit in peace."

David appeared uncharacteristically shaken by what had happened. He insisted, and I didn't doubt his truthfulness, that he had not so much as even read any of the Enochian Calls before that evening.

For the next three years, we would hold class *two* nights a week and focus exclusively on Enochian magick. We would depend increasingly on *The Complete Enochian Dictionary* to help us navigate the complexities of the angelic hierarchies and serve as our pronunciation guide to angelic language. David's visions would continue to take us on amazing excursions to the Elemental worlds, but as he became more accustomed to hearing the words of the Calls his talent for breaking spontaneously into the angelic tongue diminished and finally ceased altogether. He remains the most talented seer I have ever encountered.

D. R., bless his heart, eventually moved away. We haven't heard from him in many years. I am forever grateful to him for bringing *The Complete Enochian Dictionary* to class that memorable night so many years ago. As you have probably guessed, I never returned it to him.

The Lost Art of
Enochian Magic

Angels, Invocations, and Secrets
Revealed to Dr. John Dee

PREFACE TO THE 2010 EDITION[1]

I was gratified beyond words when Dr. DeSalvo asked me to pen a few words for his marvelous work. I can say without hesitation that the reader is in for an exciting, provocative, and enlightening experience; for some of you it may also be the beginning of an adventurous journey of self-discovery.

It is a work that I believe could only have been written in the morning hours of the twenty-first century, when advanced scientific thought is promising us an unprecedented understanding of the cosmos and the nature of matter and energy. As our astro and quantum physicists draw closer to the Holy Grail of a theory to explain it all, can it be possible that we are approaching a level of inquiry so profound that we will soon be required to dramatically expand our level of consciousness in order to process the multidimensional answers?

I believe the answer is "Yes," and as we penetrate ever deeper into these new frontiers of thought, we are

---

1 Written for John DeSalva, PhD, *The Lost Art of Enochian Magic: Angels, Invocations, and Secrets Revealed to Dr. John Dee,* Rochester, Vermont: Destiny Books, 2010.

confronted with the same fundamental issues and challenges that have faced *spiritual* scientists since the dawn of human consciousness: How was the universe created? How can it be limitless? What sustains it? Will it ever end—if so, how? What is the nature of time, space, reality, and consciousness? Who and what am I? Try as it might to do otherwise, when her musings soar to these heights science is forced by the limitations of word-images to evoke the metaphoric language of mythology, mysticism and magic in her attempt to even *discuss* these transcendent matters.

Why, then, should it be thought unscientific for us to explore these same issues directly by magical means? After all, for tens of thousands of years of human history, right up to the eighteenth century, magic *was* science. Magic[2] is the mother of mathematics, astronomy, biology, chemistry, architecture, and medicine. It does us no good to argue that mythology, mysticism, and magic are irrational and illogical, for indeed, the mysteries of astrophysics and quantum mechanics appear to be so as well.

For the better part of a thousand years, adepts of the Holy Kabbalah[3] (Judaism's esoteric science of the soul) have by means of a variety of curious techniques endeavored to use the mind to transcend the mind. For the sake of convenience, they view "God" as the absolute and supreme consciousness of the universe, and individual humans as miniature reflections of the supreme consciousness—"Man made in the image of God." Just as my reflection in the bathroom mirror 'lives'

---

2 Sometimes spelled, "magick" to distinguish it the spiritual art from that of the stage magician.
3 The word is based upon three Hebrew letters, Qoph, Lamed, Daleth, it is often rendered, "Qabalah," "Qabala," "Cabala," "Kabalah" or "Kabbalah".

only because of my living presence, so too do I exist as a reflected unit of the supreme consciousness. My seeming separation from God is as illusionary a phenomenon as my reflection in the mirror mistakenly believing itself real and somehow estranged from the physical me on the other side of the looking glass.

Because God and humans are two aspects of the same consciousness, the Kabbalists view us both as being divided (categorized would be a better word) into four main levels of consciousness:

- The lowest level (as an aspect of the supreme consciousness) is the *material plane* itself.

   - Specific example: a rocking chair.

   - For us (as an aspect of the individual consciousness) this level manifests as our physical bodies.

- The next level (as an aspect of the supreme consciousness) is the *formative plane* where exist the patterns of everything that will manifest on the material plane.

   - Specific example: the idea or concept of a rocking chair. The Kabbalists call this the world of Angels.

   - For us (as an aspect of the individual consciousness) this level is our intellect—our mind's eye.

- Above this (as an aspect of the supreme consciousness) is the *creative plane* where the great
general principals of the universe are generated.

  - Specific example: the concept of sitting
    down. The Kabbalists call this the world of
    Archangels.

  - For us (as an aspect of the individual con-
    sciousness) this level manifests as mysterious
    powers of intuition, i.e., when a mother
    awakes in the night when her child has
    been in an accident far away—an ability
    that transcends logic and time and space.

- Above this (as an aspect of the supreme consciousness) is the *archetypal plane*—for all intents
and purposes we could consider this the consciousness of godhead itself.

  - Specific example: the universal concept of
    rest.

  - For us (as an aspect of the individual con-
    sciousness) is the life force itself—ultimately
    our true identity.

In the metaphoric language of Hebrew mysticism,
the mechanics of creation and the cooperative symphony
of all the natural forces of the cosmos are a well-ordered
hierarchy of spiritual agencies—archangels, angels, spirits, and demons. We also have our special place in this
hierarchy, and a special duty to perform. As humans, living on the material plane, we are the culmination of the

process. We resonate with a full collection of the echoes of the entire creational cycle. Each of us, as a monad of the supreme consciousness, is a tuning fork vibrating as the pure *lower harmonic* of the absolute *note*.

It is the job (indeed, I believe it is the destiny) of each of us to raise our consciousness step-by-step, octave by octave, back up to godhead. This is the true initiatory adventure each one of us are destined undergo. This is the Great Work.

One branch of Kabbalistic philosophy views the cycle of the descent into matter and return journey home as a *ten step* process; the roadmap being a schematic diagram called the *Tree of Life*. Enochian vision magic of Dr. John Dee, however, divides the trip not into ten levels, but into *thirty*, and it is the step-by-step exploration of these thirty Aethyrs or heavens of human/divine consciousness that is the fascinating subject of Dr. DeSalvo's bold and visionary experiences.

PART SIX

MAGICAL MASONRY

~~~~~~~~~~~~~~~~~~~~~~~~~~~~~~~~

My father, Clifford Ernest DuQuette, was perhaps the most honest and noble human being I have ever known. He was not at all interested in Magick and wasn't a "religious" person per se, but he was defined by an almost mystical standard of moral integrity. He was good man . . . and he was good for goodness sake . . . not because of any particular religious doctrine or belief, but rather, he was good because he knew in his heart that "being good" was the natural and human way to live. He joined the Masons in 1948, the year I was born, and I believe Masonry was the cornerstone of his character.

Freemasonry

Ritual, Symbols and History
of the Secret Society

FOREWORD TO THE 2007 EDITION[1]

*Masonry is a progressive moral science, divided into
different degrees; and, as its principles and mystic
ceremonies are regularly developed and illustrated,
it is intended and hoped that they will make a deep
and lasting impression upon your mind.*

—THE FELLOW CRAFT DEGREE
FREE AND ACCEPTED MASONS[2]

It's 4:00 A.M. I creep quietly passed the rooms of my
sleeping Brothers and out to the darkened hallway
that leads to the staircase to the Atrium. The Atrium
is a cavernous space, nearly two hundred feet long and
over fifty feet wide, built in the style of the Roman
Empire. The marble floor is adorned with Masonic
symbols inlayed in brass and stone of contrasting colors.
The Doric and Ionic columns that flank the great hall
and support second story walkways and chambers are
dwarfed by towering Corinthian columns that buttress

---

1   Written for Mark Stavish, *Freemasonry: Ritual, Symbols and History of the Secret
    Society,* Rochester,Vermont: Destiny Books, 2010.
2   From the *California Cipher,* Grand Lodge of California, F. & A.M. San
    Francisco: Allen Publishing Company, 1990.

the vaulted ceiling, three stories high, whose center-piece stained glass skylight now bathes the room in soft iridescent moonlight.

There are five statues here whose bronze presences I am moved to honor. Four are the goddess figures of the *Cardinal Virtues*, Temperance, Prudence, Fortitude, and Justice. They are positioned at the corners of the room which I slowly circumambulate as I move from pedestal to pedestal. The fifth goddess stands in the very center of the hall and bears no inscription or emblem. She simply holds her forefinger to her lips as if to hush the universe. It is here at the feet of silence I sit down on the cool floor and close my eyes. Only a moment, it seems, passes before I hear the warm ring of a temple bowl. The others are awake, and we are being called to dawn meditation.

I slip off my shoes outside the door of the lodge room and tiptoe inside and take my seat. The room is dark save for a single candle on the central altar. After a few quiet words of introduction and instruction we close our eyes and enter our inner temples. Forty min-utes later the sun has risen. We open our eyes and see the room brilliantly illuminated by three large Italian stain glass panels that we now see forms the entire south-ern wall of the lodge room. Each window dramatically depicts one of the *three ages of man*—youth, manhood, and old age. My eyes linger on each scene in turn as I weigh the well-lived episodes of my life against those of time misspent.

After breakfast we gather beneath chandeliers of Czechoslovakian crystal in the spacious reception room and for the first time see who has come this year. I immediately recognize some of the brightest stars in the firmament of modern Masonry. I also see friends and colleagues from years passed, writers, scholars, teachers and students. As always, there are several Brothers who have been invited for the first time to present papers and lecture.

We are met for three days of presentations and discussions of issues and subjects relating to esoteric aspects of the Craft of Freemasonry. We have gathered secretly and informally under no official warrant, charter or auspices, to explore the Craft as a self-transformational art and science—gathered to labor and strategize how best to proceed to protect, preserve and advance the esoteric soul of Freemasonry.

Appropriately, the venue for this gathering is one of the largest and most architecturally magnificent Masonic edifices in the world, *unexplainably* abandoned by its usual team of custodial stewards for the duration of our meetings. The building itself is intoxicating. We are all humbled by its beauty and perfect proportions. One cannot resist being tangibly elevated as we each intuitively attempt to adjust our inner imperfections to reflect the outer perfections of the sacred geometry around us. As we walk the sacred labyrinth, or sit quietly studying in the gothic library, or muse about alchemy at the feet of Assyrian sphinxes, we find ourselves pausing and asking each other, "Is this really happening?"

Yes. It really happens; and *this* is how I always dreamed Masonry would be.

This, however, is not what all Masons think the Craft should be. As a matter of fact, there are a great many who now feel that the esoteric roots of our ancient institution are an embarrassment—queer and unwholesome links to paganism, the occult, and perhaps even Satanism. You might be surprised to learn that there is a concerted effort now taking place within Masonry to once and for all divorce the Craft from its esoteric heritage, and make it an organization open only to men professing certain specific religious convictions. Even though Masonic tradition dictates that a candidate need only profess a belief in a Supreme Being and a form of afterlife, today there are jurisdictions and lodges around the world that will not consider the application of a man if they believe his religion to be not "mainstream" enough, or his interest in the esoteric nature of the craft suspiciously intense.

This is why, sadly, I cannot tell you in what country our gathering takes place. Neither can I tell you the names of the participants, or the circumstances that bring us together, or the details of our activities and goals. By necessity Masonry has for us again become a secret society.

What makes this anti-esoteric movement so ill-timed and suicidal is the fact that Masonry's membership numbers are plunging precipitously. Lodges are closing or merging with other lodges for lack of members. Freemasonry, as we've known it for the last three hundred years will be dead in just a few years if something isn't done. Ironically (and much to the terror of the anti-esoterics) the *only* demographic group that is applying for membership in significant numbers is composed of young men who are passionately interested in the esoteric mysteries of the Craft.

Fortunately, at least for the time being, exoteric Masonry is still for the most part a very big tent. Even in the most conservative quarters leadership still pays lip service to the concept that Masonry opens her doors to upstanding men[3] of all races, religions, political persuasions and social and economic circumstances. Aside from the obligatory duties required to advance through the degrees, the individual Mason is free to be as interested or as disinterested as he likes in matters that concern the history, rituals, traditions, and mysteries of the Craft. As it is (and much to the relief of the anti-esoterics), most Masons, once they are raised to the Sublime Degree of Master Mason (and, if they so choose, go on to complete the degrees in one or more concordant rites) are happy to put the *quaint and curious* stuff behind them and simply enjoy being part of one of the most active and generous service organizations in the world.

This is as it should be, and please don't think that I am denigrating the contributions and efforts of a Brother who wishes to participate at any level. The world needs a generous service organization to sponsor hospitals and clinics and scholarships. Some men need a relatively wholesome place to meet socially once or twice a month with other relatively wholesome men. Add to this the possibility that some men might actually have a psychological need to put on clown make-up and drive tiny cars in parades.

Without men like this Masonry would not be (for the time being at least) the largest and wealthiest fraternal organization in the world. These are good men who *are* made better by their involvement in Craft. But there are also those among them who would like to be spiritually transformed by Masonry's deeper secrets; and

---

3 Although there are several organizations such as "Co-Masonry" that accepts both men and woman, and other rites that are exclusive to women, "Regular" Masonry remains for the present a men's fraternity.

currently these are the only men applying in any significant numbers. (Still, I'd wager that even some of the clowns in the tiny cars, if properly educated, might be fascinated by the esoteric side of things.)

The sad fact is most Masons are never adequately exposed to knowledgeable Brothers or material that might excite their curiosity beyond wondering, "What's for Stated Meeting dinner?" It's not that the information is not available. Plenty of fine books have been written over the centuries, some of which might be found in the libraries of local lodges all around the world. But many of these books were written in the 1800s at a time when interest in esoteric Masonry was at its zenith and when even a high school diploma meant a familiarity with Greek and Latin and a smattering of philosophy, world religions, and history. Anyone who has ever started to read Albert Pike's *Morals and Dogma*,[4] will know exactly what I'm talking about.

What has been lacking for the modern Mason, and what Brother Stavish now mercifully presents us, is a straightforward, and step-by-step, study of Freemasonry and the myriad movements and ideas that gave birth to Craft in all its manifestations. Moreover, he sets it all *vis á vis* 21st century science, philosophy, and mysticism and challenges the reader to do the same. *The Path of Freemasonry* is a one-volume liberal arts education in Freemasonry, and never before in the history of the Craft has it been more important for individual Masons to be so educated. I wish I could put Brother Stavish's book in the hands of every newly-raised Brother, not simply for his own benefit, but for the benefit of those

---

4   Pike, Albert. *Morals and Dogma of the Ancient and Accepted Scottish Rite of Freemasonry,* Washington, DC: The Supreme Council of the Southern Jurisdiction.

individuals throughout his life who will look to him as worthy example of a knowledgeable and enlightened member of the Fraternity.

May the blessing of Heaven rest upon us and all regular Masons! May Brotherly Love prevail, and every moral and social virtue cement us! Amen.

—THE MASTER'S CLOSING PRAYER
FREE & ACCEPTED MASONS[5]

5   From the *California Cipher*, Grand Lodge of California, F. & A. M., Richmond, Utah: Allen Publishing Company, 1990.

Mozart, Magick, and Masonry

PRE-PERFORMANCE ADDRESS[1] TO THE 2002 OPENING
NIGHT[2] PERFORMANCE OF THE LOS ANGELES OPERA

[Spoken in Lon's best movie trailer voice]

*In a world . . . where your mother is a homicidal
Moon Goddess . . .*

And your father is a Sun Worshipping Cult Leader,

*Your only protection just may be a very confused
Prince with a flute . . . .*

*And a guy dressed up like a bird . . . with a
glockenspiel !*

I'm Lon DuQuette. I'm very proud to say I'm a Mason.
My father was a Mason. My brother is a Mason. Many of
the men whose lives and works have inspired, enlightened and encouraged me throughout my life have been
Masons.

Masonry is one of the oldest (if not *the* oldest) sec-
ular fraternities in the world. It traces its *modern* origin
to 1717 when a grand lodge was formed from several

1 Copyright © 2002 Lon Milo DuQuette
2 Dorothy Chandler Pavilion, Los Angeles Music Center, March 24, 2002.

existing lodges in London. Just how long those lodges had been in existence *prior* to 1717 is unclear. There are some one hundred and thirty versions of Masonic documents known as the *Old Charges* that date from around 1390—but Masonic *tradition* would have us trace its origins back much farther—back to the medieval cathedral builder's trade unions—back to the Dionysian Artificers who built the great civic monuments of the Roman Empire—back to the builders of King Solomon's temple—even to the craftsmen who built the Great Pyramids of Egypt.

Of course, there is no real evidence to support the existence of a prehistoric International Brotherhood of Pyramid Builders (Local #327).

But, even if *none* of the *traditional* histories of the Craft can stand the scrutiny of historians, it is clear that Freemasonry, as an *initiatory* society, is an incarnation *of* (if not the heir *to*) the great mystery schools of antiquity—especially those that flourished in and around the Mediterranean basin—the Eleusinians, the rites of Mendes, of Osiris, Isis, Dionysus, Serapis, Mithras, and the Persian Magi, from whence we get the word *Magic.*

The Mystery Schools taught that, ultimately, the true essence of each man and woman is *divine* . . . in fact, if ever we could come to the full realization of our true natures we would discover we are one and the same with the supreme consciousness and life-force of the universe.

Among the various Mystery rites, the *name* and symbolic *character* of the *deity* chosen to represent this supreme consciousness varied considerably—but they all had one very important thing in common. They all surmised that it is possible to consciously raise oneself to supreme realization—and they attempted to assist this evolutionary process by degrees—by means of a step-by-step program of purification and instruction. *And* by literally *mutating* the candidate's character by putting him or her through a series of dramatic and artfully choreographed personal ordeals.

In the early years of the Christian era, Alexandria Egypt was center of the intellectual, philosophical, and initiatory world. The universal order and stability of the Roman Empire brought the world together as never before. For a brief and brilliant moment in time, knowledge and wisdom gleaned from scores of cultures from China and India to Egypt, Israel, Europe and Britain, synthesized within three great libraries. Here the holy wisdom of the Hebrew qabalah met the celestial sciences of the Chaldean Astronomers and the occult wisdom of the Egyptian priests of Isis. Here the subtleties of Taoist and Buddhist philosophies touched the mathematical sciences and pragmatic politics of the Greeks.

A catastrophic fire destroyed much of at least one of Alexandria's great libraries, and the growth and often violent zeal of the young Christian movement for all intents and purposes put an end to the overt activities of the Mystery schools. Carl Sagan speculated that, had the wealth of information stored in Alexandria not been destroyed—the level of technology that placed a man on the moon in the *20th* century would have been reached in the 1500s.

Be that as it may, we know there survived throughout the suffocating centuries of the Dark Ages, a body of men who, because of their unique knowledge and skills, formed a distinct class of *world citizen*. Men who could move freely from town to town, city to city, kingdom to kingdom —unrestricted by the limits of feudal servitude.

Masters of geometry and construction, who could make stone rise to heaven. Master artists who could enshrine the symbolic and mathematical secrets of creation within the very dimensions and ornaments of buildings that would stand for a thousand years.

These were Free-*masons*. Men who, by virtue of their own talents, wit, and experience, had freed themselves from the tyranny of kings and the oppression of the Church.

The Freemason was the *archetype* for the modern, liberated human being.

Freemasons were quite literally . . . the *coolest* guys in the western world.

When the great cathedral projects ended, the fraternity evolved from being one that applied its mystical principals upon stone, to one that does so upon the hearts of human beings. By 1784, when Wolfgang Amadeus Mozart became a Mason, the progressive Masonic ideals of Love, Tolerance, Enlightenment and Universal Brotherhood were poised to set Europe and America on fire with revolution.

Late in 1790 Mozart learned Masonry would soon be outlawed in Austria. He conspired with a Brother Mason, librettist and theatre owner, Emanuel Schikaneder, to enshrine the essence of Masonic ideals within a lighthearted (and seemingly innocuous) opera. That opera, of course, is *The Magic Flute.* And like all of Mozart's creations, it is constructed on many levels.

The first level is purely musical. By this point in Mozart's career he was famous for creating melodies that were not only beautiful to the ear, but memorable to the mind. Mozart wrote music you could hum and whistle. His musical logic is so clean and natural that the listener's ear anticipates *each* upcoming phrase as if the music is gushing spontaneously from our own mind. Mozart's audiences frequently became so instantly infected by these almost *deja-vu* melodies that they joined in with the principals on second and subsequent refrains.

The music of The Magic Flute *is* delightful, and I'm sure there was no doubt in Mozart's mind that once it was heard it would be impossible to erase it from the musical consciousness of the world.

The next level was that of contemporary comment. Several of the characters in *The Magic Flute* were quite recognizable caricatures of some of the most important and powerful people of the day:

- The darkly passionate and vengeful *Queen of the Night* was the perfect image of Empress Maria Theresia whose opposition to the ideals of the Enlightenment and hatred for Masonry was well known.

- Our hero, Tamino, was clearly based upon Emperor Joseph II, the son of Maria Theresia, who was not only a driving force of the Enlightenment, but also an early activist for equality between the classes and the sexes. Tamino's efforts, early in the opera, to please the Queen of the Night is a touching comment on the efforts of a royal son, who, in his youth, naturally made efforts to please his imperious mother.

- And Sarastro, the Wise and Noble Hierophant of the Temple of *Isis un Osiris,* could only have been Vienna's most revered Grand Master of Masons, Ignaz von Born. Von Born was the most idealized example of the Enlightened man—humanitarian, scientist, and teacher.

The next level is more esoteric and Masonic; and here we ask, does *The Magic Flute* actually reveal Masonic "Secrets?"

Technically. . . . No.

Masonic secrets concern themselves primarily with the clap-trap of the fraternity—the signs of recognition . . . the handshakes . . . passwords . . . and, of course, the details of the dramatic ceremonies of initiation. There are very few aspects of *The Magic Flute* that would worry any Mason who actually knows what is (and what is not) secret in the Craft.

Johann Wolfgang von Goethe, also a Freemason, said of *The Magic Flute*;

"It is enough that the crowd would find pleasure in seeing the spectacle; at the same time, its high significance will not escape the initiates."

In the time we have left before we enjoy tonight's performance, I'd like to highlight just a few of those elements of *high significance* that do not escape initiates.

Let's begin by observing Mozart's use of the number three. The number three is, for a number of reasons, a highly significant number to Masons. The overture of *The Magic Flute* exploits quite dramatically three chords sounded in batteries of three. These same three chords are sounded in the Temple scenes. As we will soon see, there are three Temples, three doors, three attendants to the Queen of the Night, three guiding angels, and three rounds of voting. Brother Mozart even wrote *The Magic*

Flute in E flat—a key that contains three flats in the key signature.

While these are interesting tidbits, they are hardly *veil-rending* expositions of Masonic secrets. In the Temple scenes, however, we will see the suggestions of many elements of secret Masonic procedure; from the way the brotherhood admits the candidate and votes upon his admission, to the various tests of fidelity, silence and secrecy—most especially, the ordeal of initiation itself.

Peeling back yet another layer of esoteric secrets, we discover that Brothers Mozart and Schikaneder incorporated key elements of the Hebrew Qabalah within the characters and plot of their opera. We must remember that mystical sciences such as Qabalah, Alchemy, and ceremonial magic were subjects of intense fascination to many Masons of 18th century, and it is not at all surprising that these two Masons-with-a-mission would want to load their masterpiece with the biggest mystical punch they could.

A fundamental concept of the Qabalah divides creation and the human soul into four levels. These four levels correspond to the four letters of the Great Name of God, which in Hebrew is spelled Yod, Heh, Vav, Heh, (Most of the non-Jewish world pronounces this Jehovah.) The dynamics that exist between and among all things represented by these four sacred letters is the focus of Qabalistic study and meditation. But if we were to simply personify Yod, Heh, Vav, Heh as family, they would have the characteristics of a Father, Mother, Son, & Daughter. If we thought of them as *royalty* they would be a King, Queen, Prince, & Princess.

The Qabalistic scenario goes something like this: If each of us really knew our true spiritual identity we would realize that we were like a King . . . a King who is the *most-awake* Being of all. But, for some reason, we have chosen to fall asleep. The King has fallen asleep and is dreaming he is the Queen of the Universe, who has fallen asleep and is dreaming she is the Prince of the Universe, who has fallen asleep and is dreaming he is a sleeping Princess.

Unenlightened humanity is just like Sleeping Beauty. We are dead to the greater reality and have completely forgotten our divine birthright. We are asleep to our true spiritual nature and are dreaming that we are trapped in a tomb of matter, and time and space. (This is just the position Princess Tamina finds herself in during the first Act of the Magic Flute.)

There is part of us, however, that is not so deeply asleep, a part of us that remembers there is something more. This *more-awake* self is our own Prince Charming. If only he could kiss our Sleeping Beauty and break the spell of illusion, then the Princess could marry the Prince and become the *even-more-awake* Queen, and by doing so the Prince will automatically be elevated to become the *most-awake* King.

The great secret to this Qabalistic soap opera is, of course, the **Zen**-like revelation that each one of us has been the *most-awake King* all along.

I know this sounds hopelessly mystical and abstract— because it *is* hopelessly mystical and abstract. It is also is the hidden scaffolding that supports and sustains the Western spiritual tradition—*and,* as such, it is naturally the plot and a subplot of *The Magic Flute.*

We have *King* Sarastro, the *Queen* of the Night, *Prince* Tamino, and *Princess* Pamina—and on a lower level we have *Papagano* and *Papagana* who in their own more mundane universe play *prince* and *princess* to Tamino and Pamina.

The most esoteric statement made by *The Magic Flute*, however, was one that shocked even the free-thinking Masons of Vienna—and proves Mozart to be a revolutionary even within a revolutionary society, and a visionary mystic among mystics.

Despite several charming and (by modern standards) incredibly *in*correct ditties about the nature of woman in earlier scenes, the opera climaxes with the duel initiation of Tamino and Pamina—a surprise ending that was very unsettling to many in the all-male Masonic fraternity.

To *initiates* this is more than just a social comment upon the equality of the sexes. It is a bold and vision-ary statement that touches upon the very dynamics of humanity's evolving consciousness.

At the beginning of the opera we meet the awe-some and beautiful Queen of the Night enthroned upon the moon. She represents a time in human history when *woman* was the supreme mystery. An innocent but primitive age when life appeared to spring directly from woman, and was linked to the cycles of the moon. This was the time of the great goddess and matriarchal social and religious institutions.

As human consciousness evolved we began to rec-ognize how important the *sun* was to life on earth, and the importance of the *man's* contribution to the procreative process. The pendulum swung violently in the opposite direction. *Patriarchies* supplanted matriar-chies, and the Great Goddess was overthrown and ruth-lessly subjugated by male gods. *This* is the source of the vengeful hatred that the *Lunar* Queen of the Night feels for Sarastro and his *sun-worshipping* order.

Mozart envisioned the *next* step in human consciousness, when equality and balance between the sexes is achieved—when the Moon and the Sun are no longer at war but *united* to bring a new light to the world.

Initiation means "a beginning." Pamina and Tamino's initiation at the end of The Magic Flute represents Mozart's sweetest hope that a new and wonderful age was at hand. An age in which the Masonic ideals of Brotherly Love, Relief, and Truth would manifest in the hearts of all humanity.

An age when, as the three Guiding Angels sing;
" . . . All doubts will disappear,
when only the wise will rule . . .
Oh heavenly peace, return to us, and fill the hearts of all.
Then the earth will a heaven seem . . .
And mortals will have godly esteem"

Well . . . It's almost time for the opera to begin. We are very lucky people. A wonderful, delightful, and *magical* initiation awaits us just inside the great doors of the temple of music; an initiation we can experience simply by seeing, hearing, and enjoying. The Ritual team is almost ready. Grand Master Plácido Domingo has consecrated the Temple; Maestro Foster and Sir Peter Hall will serve tonight as Junior and Senior Wardens; and our Worshipful Master in the East will be none other than the immortal spirit of Wolfgang Amadeus Mozart.

Thank you very much. Enjoy your evening.

PART SEVEN

MAGICAL MISCELLANY

~~~~~~

Each of us slumbers in a dream uniquely our own.
So then, each of us must awaken in our own unique way.

—unpublished fragments of the
wisdom of Rabbi Lamed Ben Clifford

Finding the Way

A Tao for
Down-to-Earth People

FOREWORD TO THE 2005 EDITION[1]

It is probably a serious breach of scholarly decorum to begin a Foreword to another author's work by writing about oneself. In this case, I hope to be forgiven for the my lapse into spiritual narcissism for, in truth, I have been touched and deeply identify with what I perceive to be the spirit of this marvelous work—a work that (if names and labels did not serve only to confuse matters) could be described as "*Western* Eastern thought."

I'm a westerner. I say this not as a boast or an apology. It's just a fact. I was born in California and raised in the Midwest. My parents were of western European and Native American stock. I was noisily raised in an archetypically dysfunctional family of good Methodists in the archetypically dysfunctional universe of 1950s-60s small-town Nebraska (advertised as the place "Where the West Begins!"). Back then there were no minority groups in town; no Jews, no Buddhists, no Hindus or Muslims. Nobody spoke about "Eastern thought" or "Western thought." As a matter of fact, in small-town Nebraska nobody spoke about "thought" at all; and, until I moved

---

1 Written for Susan Montag, *Finding the Way: A Tao for Down-to-Earth People*, Lake Worth, Florida: Nicolas Hays, 2005.

back (west) to California to go to college, I believed that the act of *not thinking about thought* was the Western way.

The psychedelic revolution of the mid 1960s radically changed my thinking on this subject and most everything else. Almost overnight, I realized with Technicolor certainty that human consciousness—my consciousness—was an awesome and holy thing, perhaps the most important thing in the universe. I wasn't in Nebraska anymore—and my newly awakened third eye turned toward the east in search of more light.

I found it almost immediately in the form of a tiny book that I bought at my college bookstore for 95 cents. It bore the curious two-part title, *Lao Tzu—Tao Te Ching*,[2] and advertised itself as ". . . the principal classic in the thought of Taoism."[3]

The translator's very lengthy and scholarly introduction was of no interest to me. My craving for instant spiritual gratification was too strong. I thumbed straight to the opening lines of the text itself and sipped my first ambrosial taste of Eastern thought.

The way that can be told
Is not the constant way;
The name that can be named
Is not the constant name.

The nameless was the beginning of heaven and earth;
The named was the mother of the myriad creatures.[4]

---

2   D.C. Lau, trans. *Lau Tzu—Tao Te Ching*, Baltimore: Penguin Books, 1963, latest reprint 1985.
3   *Ibid.* Back cover material.
4   *Ibid.* p. 57.

What beauty! It was perfect—so perfectly simple; forty words describing what cannot be described—the infinitely simple, nameless *Way Things Are*. Forget about Deities or Saviors or Devils or sin or guilt or reward or punishment. Those are things with names, and names separate everything from the pure, nameless *Way Things Are*.

For a moment I stopped breathing. It was as if I had ingested a spiritual drug and was pausing to see if I would explode, or turn purple, or die, or giggle.

Of course, I didn't do any of those things (well, maybe I giggled a little). After a few months of reading and re-reading the text and meditating upon its inscrutable words, I resolve to discard completely the faith of my fathers and try my hand at becoming a first rate Eastern mystic. For a few years I didn't do such a bad job. I left the world of psychedelics, started seriously practicing yoga and the obligatory meditative practices, and began a systematic study of the *I Ching*.

Yes sir, I had great spiritual goals. I was going to be egoless. I was going to be the most egoless mystic in town. I envisioned my egoless self quietly gaining illumination while poised egolessly by the coy pond, my legs locked in a flawless lotus position, my eyes firmly fixed upon the center of my egoless forehead, my shaved head gleaming in the leaf-filtered sunlight of my cool and tranquil Zen garden.

Man! I was going to look *so cool* without an ego!

Obviously, something wasn't right, and it was more than just my battle with the ego. It was a battle with how I was hardwired. It was as though I was trying to run eastern software on my western hardware. It was then I began to examine the nature of my western psyche and the differences between the eastern and western approaches to enlightenment.

No matter what some of the pundits of each school may preach, the goals are the same; supreme illumination and absorption into godhead. But the ways the eastern and western mystic go about achieving that goal are as different as Yin and Yang—In and Out.

The spiritual sciences of the east encourage the individual to simplify—to turn *inward* to discover the true nature of self and Deity. By stilling the body and mind, and systematically striping away the illusionary veils of sensations, desires and ego, the eastern mystic eventually reaches the moment when something snaps—the mind is transcended, and he or she is absorbed into what is poorly described as wall-to-wall *emptiness*.

Conversely, by nature western mystics are inclined to seek *externally* for the answers. Consider how we in the west are so obedient to scripture and complex doctrines—so attracted to ritual, priest crafts, and prayerful appeals to a God apparently outside of ourselves and nature. Under the right circumstances, however, these outward things can trigger in the devotee an illumination that "fills the soul" with the presence of deity—something snaps—the mind is transcended, and the consciousness of the western mystic is absorbed into what can be poorly described as wall-to-wall *fullness*.

Realizing that that the two supreme goals are one and the same—that subjective reality lives in objective things and actions left me in a most awkward and frustrating position—the lonesome, inside-out schizophrenia of the *Western* Eastern mystic. Fortunately I would eventually bring this malady under control by heavily self-medicating myself with the concepts and practices of the *Zen of the West*; the Hermetic[5] Qabalah, Tarot and ceremonial magick.

These highly esoteric western traditions are not for everyone. Indeed, for centuries they have been branded as heretical by the western spiritual "authorities" who have (for reasons both understandable and despicable) either found themselves unable to appreciate the subtleties of the practices, or else have been frustrated in their attempts to successfully exploit the practices for profit or crowd control. If not for my background in Eastern thought, I too would have dismissed the mystic arts of the West as dangerous and superstitious nonsense.

All this being said, it remains a mystery why as a meat-and-potatoes midwestern Methodist teenager I was immediately and profoundly zapped by the *Tao Te Ching,* or why for the most part my zeal to share its wisdom with others of my occidental ilk met with no success at all.

"Don't you get it?" became my mantra of frustration.

"No. I don't. It's just fortune cookie double talk. How can I believe in that?"

"It's not something you *believe* in, it's the *way things are!*"

"What's so holy about things they way they are?

"No. Not about things the *way they are* . . . it's about the *way.* Don't you get it? Focusing on the *things* is how everything got all screwed up."

"I don't get it. How's that going to get me into heaven!"

(Insert sound of my hand slapping my own forehead here.)

---

5 Spelled Qabalah to differentiate it from its overtly parochial cousins, the Hebrew Kabbalah or the Christian Cabala.

Obviously, it's almost impossible to be an enthusiastic proselytizer of the *Tao* without departing embarrassingly far from the *way* the moment one opens one's mouth. Handing a curious friend or a relative a translation (even a very good translation) is at best a hit or miss affair. For thirty-five years I've bemoaned the fact that someone, some *Western* Eastern mystic with a masterful grasp of spirit of the text and the ability to render it into straightforward, down-to-earth English, has not done the job.

I lament no longer. I have found the English language jewel I've been seeking my entire adult life—a jewel I can share with everyone I know who insists they *don't get it.*

Exactly how she did it I cannot say. However, one thing is abundantly clear to me. By writing *Finding the Way* Susan Montag has demonstrated in the clearest, most comfortable manner imaginable that she has truly *found the Way.*

The New Hermetics

21st Century Magick for Illumination and Power

FOREWORD TO THE 2004 EDITION[1]

There's not the smallest orb which thou behold'st

But in his motion like an angel sings,

Still quiring to the young-ey'd cherubins;

Such harmony is in immortal souls;

But whilst this muddy vesture of decay

Doth grossly close it in, we cannot hear it.

LORENZO TO JESSICA
THE MERCHANT OF VENICE, IV, 1

To slip the muddy vesture of decay, in which essence of our immortal soul like a sleeping princess lies entombed, is the Great Work. It is the Sacred Quest of the mystic, alchemist, yogi, and magician, but it is also the inescapable destiny of every unit of evolving consciousness in the universe.

---

1 Written for Jason Augustus Newcomb, *The New Hermetics: 21st Century Magick for Illumination and Power,* Newburyport, Massachusetts: Weiser Books, 2004.

But how do we go about extricating this pristine essence from the tomb that so "grossly" closes us in? Can we chip it away like a clay cocoon? Can we shed it like a serpent's skin? Can we wash ourselves clean of it?

We can try. Indeed, plotting the escape from this prison of matter is the *raison d'être* of the world's great religions. As Hindus and Buddhists we deny it as illusion; as Christians we attempt to bribe our way free with a ransomed savior; and together with the other 'people of the Book—Muslims and Jews—we hate and fear it like a devil; make war upon it like an enemy; flee from it like sin and (discarding God-given common sense) gamble our souls on the historicity of myths and obedience to scriptural law so that after death we might discover we have won the prize of immortality.

Such efforts in-and-of themselves will remain forever doomed, for while they are effective instruments for spiritual crowd-control they ignore one very fundamental and paradoxical cosmic truth. That is, the tomb of matter, the "muddy vesture of decay," is *itself* an inextricable part of the essence of our immortal soul. For is it not written that *the temple of initiation is also a tomb?*

HERMETICS—OLD AND NEW

I am particularly pleased and honored Mr. Newcomb has asked me to pen the foreword to this remarkable book—remarkable in that it offers more than musings and the retelling of ancient material—remarkable in that he demonstrates so pleasantly that one can focus intensely upon the mystery teachings of the past without isolating oneself from the discoveries and revelations of the present—that one can unite the modern sciences of the mind with the wonder and wisdom of the ages.

It is a labor not too dissimilar to the works of a number of individuals who in the twilight of the golden ages of Egypt and Greece shared their wisdom in a body of mystical texts supposedly written by the God Thoth, or Hermes, or Hermes Trismagistos. Foremost among these is one that bears the name of its mythical author, *The Emerald Tablet of Hermes*. Tradition maintains it was the first revelation of God to mankind—that it was cast in liquid emerald by the magick of alchemy, its raised letters revealing in thirteen short verses the universal operations of nature. It is the famous work that gave us the fundamental Hermetic axiom;

> It is true and no lie, certain, and to be
> depended upon, that the superior agrees with
> the inferior, and the inferior with superior, to
> effect that one truly wonderful work.[2]

Verses five and six go on to provide the diligent aspirant the mystic key by which he or she can arise from the tomb of matter even while acknowledging the tomb is an integral part of the self.

> The power is perfect, after it has been united
> with a spirituous earth. Separate the spirituous
> earth from the dense or crude earth by means
> of a gentle heat, with much attention.[3]

---

2 Manly P. Hall, *Lost Keys of Freemasonry*, Richmond, Virginia: Macoy, 1968, p. 96.
3 Ibid.

It is the profoundest of cosmic ironies. The divine power, our true spiritual essence, does not achieve perfection until it hits the "rock bottom" of the cosmos—the dense and crude earth. It remains *im*perfect until the moment of entombment for the simple reason that until that dark nadir is reached the experiential adventure of existence remains incomplete, and Self is not yet endowed with the entire spectrum of the light of consciousness—from spirit to matter—from the highest high to the lowest low.

This is why Hermetic tradition informs us the highest the angelic hosts envy the children of the dust because humans have something they will never have—a little bit of everything from top to bottom. High as they are, the angels are stuck in divine middle management without a complete stash of the raw material necessary to clone themselves to perfect godhead. Aleister Crowley describes this processes as " . . . *the general doctrine that the climax of the Descent into Matter is the signal for the redintegration[4] by Spirit.* "[5] Once the lowest low has been reached, *the power is perfect* and the process of return is initiated.

The *Emerald Tablet of Hermes* tells us how to begin. We are to, "Separate the spirituous earth from the dense or crude earth by means of a gentle heat, with much attention." This doesn't mean we are to cook ourselves over a low flame (Although in the symbolic language of Alchemy that's pretty much what we do.). It means that through a slow, balanced and gentle process we are to (with great attention) distill the essence of our being, the song of our soul, from the *muddy vesture of decay.*

---

4   Redintegration is an archaic word meaning "*restoration to a former state.*"
5   *The Book of Thoth* by The Master Therion (Aleister Crowley). A Short Essay on the Tarot of the Egyptians, London: O.T.O., 1944. The Equinox III (5). Reprinted York Beach, Maine, Samuel Weiser, 1992, p. 89.

This is the initiatory process of the Hermeticist old and new—a balanced and gentle program of study, practice, meditation, mixed with the effects of one's own inherited destiny (whether you call that luck, good fortune, or karma).

Initiation is not a reward for achievement or seal of attainment. Indeed, the initiate may never attain (at least not in this incarnation). "Initiation" means *to begin,* and the first question the candidate is asked at the threshold of the Temple is simply, "Are you ready to begin?"

Are you? If so, I can think of no better place to start than the marvelous book you hold in your hands right now—a balanced and gentle program of study, practice and meditation. To this you must add the most important ingredient of all—yourself—the sum total of the highest high and the lowest low—your inherited destiny.

The Art and Practice of Geomancy

Divination, Magic, and Earth Wisdom of the Renaissance

FOREWORD TO THE 2009 EDITION[1]

"Seek earth, and heaven shall be added unto you!"

FRANCIS BENDICK[2]

"I love the earth."

The driver pretended he didn't hear me. From the moment he collected me at the airport in Bristol he allowed me to sit silently and be seduced by the charm and splendor of southwest England's green and pleasant pastures. Radstock, near Bath in Somerset was my destination. It was an area of the UK I never visited before so I had no idea how long I would be able to savor my chauffeured religious experience.

Never had I seen so many shades of green in my life. It felt like I was living inside the swelling phrases of Blake's great national hymn, *Jerusalem*. A "countenance

---

1 Written for John Michael Greer, *The Art and Practice of Geomancy: Divination, Magic, and Earth Wisdom of the Ranaissance*, Newburyport, Massachusetts: Weiser Books, 2009.

2 Francis Bendick (Aleister Crowley). *The Earth*. The Equinox I (6), London, Fall, 1911. Reprint York Beach, Maine: Weiser Books, 1992. Supplement, p. 110.

divine" did indeed shine forth upon these clouded hills. This was heaven on earth. No. This was heaven *of* earth.

I rolled down the window and inhaled the perfume of grass and soil warmed by the sun of mid July.

"I love the earth." I said again, this time under my breath.

I closed my eyes as if to take a snapshot of the moment, and was surprised to feel a tear burst over the lower lash of my right eye and coolly evaporate in the wind as it ran down my cheek. I assure you, in my jaded heart such sensitive moments are a rarity, and usually occur only in the fleeting seconds that follow the first and second sip of a late afternoon martini.[3] This day's rapture was most likely induced by the stress and debauchery of visiting five countries in seven days, and the realization that after this lecture I'd be returning home to my own bed. Whatever the cause, I was drunk on earth and wished the driver would stop the car so that I might stretch out in a field and soak the verdant ground with my tears of love.

The mental image of such an awkward and unseemly act immediately erased such daydreams, but for the first time in my life I realized deep down to the very core of my soul that the earth is a living, breathing, conscious being—an intelligence—a god(dess)—and that I was her child. My flesh her soil and mantle; my blood her rivers and streams and seas; my bones her stones and mountains; my heartbeat her molten core—my soul one with her soul.

What more palpable deity could humanity seek? What god more wonderful, more worthy of our awe, our gratitude, our prayers? We must certainly honor the

---

3 Regrettably this pure bliss disappears around the third and fourth sip.

sun as the ultimate source of light and life, but without earth to reflect the solar glory, without the earth and her manifold creatures Sol Invictus would remain eternally a god unworshipped.

Moreover, is not the earth herself sunlight made manifest? Earth is the climax of spirit's descent into matter—the magical lowest low that contains not only a spark of the highest high but everything else in between. Earth is the alchemical laboratory that transmutes light into life. Earth is the crowning finale of creation, and we are conscious creatures of the earth. As such, you and I possess—we embody—the secret of spirit's return to godhead. As it is written in the *Emerald Tablet of Hermes*, "That *One Only Thing* (after God) is the father of all things in the universe. Its power is perfect, after it has been united to a spirituous earth."[4]

It is humanity's most ancient and self-evident fact of life—the sun is our father, the earth is our mother—and no matter how gender-neutral our culture may strive to become, it is the mother who first hears our cries. It is the mother who first responds to our needs. It is the mother who first answers our questions.

How ironic it is, then, that as we grow into head-strong youngsters we become less and less inclined to listen to the voice our mother. As hormone-blinded adolescents we embarrassedly shun her counsel and ridicule her prophetic warnings regarding the dire consequences of our shortsightedness and foolish behavior. As self-absorbed young adults we shut our minds completely to the possibility she could in any way understand what *our* life is like, or what is or is not in our best interest. It is not until we have reached a significant level

---

4   Manly P. Hall, *Lost Keys of Freemasonry,* Richmond, Virginia: Macoy, 1968, p. 96.

maturity that we realize that we've been blessed since birth with our own personal omniscient oracle, one whose unconditional love for us is beyond all human comprehension.

For centuries the art of geomancy has been a proper and respectful means by which we, as children of the earth, purposefully affirm our recognition of the earth as a living intelligence capable of answering our questions. The techniques and apparatus have varied from century to century, culture to culture, but its oracular vocabulary of sixteen geomantic figures (each made up of one or two dots neatly stacked four high) have remained constant.

My introduction to the art of geomancy came in 1974 when I purchased a tiny book by Israel Regardie titled *A Practical Guide to Geomantic Divination*.[5] Its size was not intimidating and Regardie's straightforward (and seemingly sane) approach to the subject made it all sound very appealing to a wide-eyed young proto-magician. An added attraction was the fact that geomancy had been (at the turn of the 20th century) a favorite oracle of the members and adepts of the Golden Dawn—and oh! how I wanted to be like one of those Golden Dawn guys!

My expectations were high, perhaps too high, for this oracle of earth. I envisioned hairy little pipe smoking gnomes popping up in my bedroom temple to grumpily answer my questions and lead me to buried treasure in the back yard. What I found was what appeared to be an abbreviated (and not very exciting) variety of astrology.

---

5   Regardie, Israel, *A Practical Guide to Geomantic Divination,* New York: Samuel Weiser, 1972.

What does astrology have to do with an earth oracle? I was really hoping for something quick and easy I could do without having to study a bunch of other stuff. Geomancy was starting to look like work.

I nevertheless gritted my teeth and dug into that tiny book. In doing so I received my first (albeit remedial) lessons on the nature and basic meaning of the planets and signs of the zodiac, and of course, the names and meanings of the sixteen geomantic figures.

I have to confess that my first attempts to divine with geomancy were (from my perspective) abysmal failures. Not only did I not know enough about astrology to get a clear answer out of the chart that my dot juggling had generated, but my interpretations of what I thought I *did* understand turned out to be patently wrong (as future events proved in objective reality).

I asked (almost forced) Constance to give it a try. She has Taurus rising in her natal chart. She's got a green-thumb in the garden. She's the darling of all animals, insects and flowers. I hoped perhaps her earthiness would be more in harmony with the art. She protested she didn't want to consult the "dirt oracle." Still, she was a good sport and reluctantly agreed to ask a question and proceeded to generate her four "mothers" by sixteen throws of tiny pebbles on the kitchen countertop. Her efforts generated the dreaded *Rubeus* in the first house. Ouch! That's bad! When that happens the book told us we were supposed to abandon the operation and not try again for hours. It's the geomantic equivalent of the gypsy fortuneteller saying, "I see nooootheeeng! Go! Now! LEEEEEVE MY TENT!"

That did it for Constance, and pretty much for me too.

It would be a dozen years before I again developed any serious interest in the art of geomancy. Again it was a book, *The Oracle of Geomancy—Techniques of Earth Divination* by Stephen Skinner,[6] that triggered my interest. It was a clear and thorough overview of the basics and much longer and more involved than Regardie's little book. Most importantly for me, it provided many helpful tables, examples, and ways one could arrive at simple answers to simple questions.

On board the geomancy train once again, I set to work to construct a "tray" specifically designed for geomantic divinations. Actually, it is a very shallow wooden box eighteen inches square and two inches deep. I lined the bottom with a thick layer of modeling clay. I eventually adorned the top and outer sides of the walls) with the sixteen geomantic symbols and the names and sigils of the spirits along with their planetary and astrological symbols. With a pointed stick I marked out sixteen horizontal bands in the clay. During geomantic operations I use the same stick to poke the random marks within the bands to arrive at the initial four Mother figures. I reserved part of the clay surface to accommodate the Mothers and the twelve other figures that they generate. The deep permanent lines on the surface of the clay make it possible to execute the figure-generating part operation entirely in clay without resorting to pencil and paper. I have to admit; it looks very magical and works marvelously well. The feeling that I am working directly with earth is powerful and unmistakable.

Finally, I had made peace with geomancy, and with the help of Skinner's book started cautiously to consult

---

6   Stephen Skinner, *The Oracle of Geomancy: Techniques of Earth Divination,*
    Bridport, Dorset, San Leandro: Prism Press, 1986.

the clay for insights on personal issues that I determined were of an "earthy" nature. I also occasionally made myself available for friends and others who come to me for quick and "dirty" geomantic readings.

Still, I was not yet a passionate devotee of the art. The works of Regardie and Skinner helped me understand how the forces, energies, intelligences, and spirits of the planets and zodiac signs could speak through the element of earth. I was comfortable enough with the theory. But neither book had sparked the flame of true spiritual *romance* in my magical soul. I had not yet connected my heart-felt love of the earth to the cold manipulations of dots on a slab of clay.

The catalyst that would eventually provide this magical link for me is the book you are now reading. When the publisher asked me if I would write this Foreword I was delighted to accept, and immediately asked them to send along the manuscript. I believe the author, John Michael Greer, to be one of the most knowledgeable and brilliant esoteric scholars alive today. He is also a friend and lodge brother whom I see far too infrequently. I do not exaggerate; I could listen to John Michael Greer talk all day and all night. His wit and insight breathes life into the movements and personalities of the dusty esoteric past. It is though he is the time-traveling custodian of the Library of Alexandria, or a medieval magician, or Renaissance magus, transported through time to share with us the brilliance and relevance of our rich spiritual ancestry.

Something 'clicked' in me when I read his historic vignettes in Chapter One. The simple, quiet charm of these little stories were for me the last alchemical ingredient in my long experiment with geomancy; the

V.I.T.R.I.O.L. that dissolved away all that previously prevented me from uniting my heart with my mind. I devoured the rest of John's magnificent book with the passion of a teenager who has just discovered poetry. As I wrote him, "It is the greatest comment on geomancy ever written." I hope you will treasure it as much as I do.

> Glory be to the Earth and to the Sun and to
> the holy body and soul of Man; and glory be
> to Love and to the Father of Love, the secret
> Unity of things!

> Also thanksgiving in the Highest for the Gift
> of all these things, and for the maiden in whom
> all these things are found, for the holy body
> and soul of man, and for the sun, and for the
> earth. AMEN.[7]

---

7   Francis Bendick (Aleister Crowley). *The Earth.* The Equinox I (6). London, Fall 1911. Reprint York Beach, Maine: Weiser Books, 1992. Supplement, p. 110.

The Weiser Book of Horror and the Occult

Hidden Magic, Occult Truths, and the Stories that Started It All

---

FOREWORD TO THE 2014 EDITION[1]

The oldest and strongest emotion of mankind is fear, and the oldest and strongest kind of fear is fear of the unknown. These facts few psychologists will dispute, and their admitted truth must establish for all time the genuineness and dignity of the weirdly horrible tale as a literary form.

H.P. LOVECRAFT—SUPERNATURAL
HORROR IN LITERATURE

"Oh, my sweet summer child," Old Nan said quietly, "what do you know of fear? Fear is for the winter, my little lord, when the snows fall a hundred feet deep and the ice wind comes howling out of the north. Fear is for the long night, when the sun hides its face for years at a time, and little children are born and live and die all in darkness while the

---

1 Written for *The Weiser Book of Horror and the Occult: Hidden Magic, Occult Truths, and the Stories that Started It All*, Newburyport, Massachusetts: Weiser Books, 2014.

*dire wolves grow gaunt and hungry, and the white
walkers move through the woods."*

GEORGE R.R. MARTIN—A GAME OF THRONES

Horror is the literature of the damned; a demon-child
art-form—conceived in the fertile depths of subconscious hell; gestated in the lonely womb of fear and
despair; brought to troubled birth by the midwife of
tortured obsessions; and reared to grotesque maturity in
the prison asylum of a terrified imagination. Horror, to
be truly horror, must be more than a frightening story.
It must be a cloistered odyssey, a claustrophobic dance
with madness. Above all, horror must be a traumatic and
soul-mutating spiritual experience—sublime, elegant,
and terrible.

Sounds disturbing, doesn't it? I hope so. Horror
should be disturbing. But, at first glance, classic horror
seldom presents itself as the product of a disturbed mind.
On the contrary, some of the best works of the genre are
introduced by narrator who seems as sane and rational
as you or I—an ordinary mind which, at the moment,
is merely grappling with extraordinary psychological
issues with which we all can more or less identify. But
beware dear reader! Your gentle empathy with the story's protagonist is a subtle poison that within a breathtakingly few paragraphs disrobes your soul and lulls you
into a poppied sleep. Naked and vulnerable (and now
uncertain of your own sanity) horror draws you irresistibly into the mind of the main character of a nightmare.

For me (or anyone who stubbornly refuses to grow
up completely) literature doesn't get better than *that*.

I turned nine years old in July of 1957, and was enduring my second melancholy summer of exile in the uncivilized[2] wilderness of Nebraska. I realize the word "exile" probably sounds melodramatic, but I was a very melodramatic child in 1957. Nebraska was for me an alien planet, cruel and hostile.

I hadn't been *born* in Nebraska. I had been kidnapped[3] by my own parents and taken there against my will. I was a Southern California boy, and I thoroughly enjoyed my first seven years in that hip and sunny fairyland where movies were made; where rock 'n' roll was evolving and the dreams and industries of the Space Age made us all feel like citizens of bright and gleaming future. The family's move to Nebraska in 1955 was in my eyes a doleful exodus back to the dark ages—a "trail of tears" from a 20th century beach paradise to a 19th century prairie hell. Powerless to change my circumstances I pouted and steeped in a bitter broth of self-absorbed discontentment.

I hated Nebraska. I hated Nebraskans. I hated the way they talked. I hated the way they laughed about butchering animals. I hated the way they preached about their wrathful God—a God who hates Negroes and Chinese (even though there wasn't a Negro or Chinese

---

2   I sincerely apologize to Nebraskans, past and present, who might be offended by my words, and ask the reader to please be mindful that my comments here about Nebraska and Nebraskans are merely giving voice to the private, personal, subjective, and immature observations of the high-strung and unhappy nine year old Lon Milo DuQuette. They do not necessarily reflect my current objective opinions of Great State of Nebraska or her remarkable and resilient citizens. I sincerely apologize to Nebraskans, past and present, who might be offended by my words.

3   Of course I wasn't actually "kidnapped." Again, my flare for the overly dramatic is getting the best of me. (That happens, especially when writing about overly dramatic subjects like horror stories.) My family moved from Southern California to Nebraska so that my father could start a new business. I was nonetheless traumatized by the move and resisted every phase of the process.

person within a hundred miles of our provincial town); a God who would condemn little boys to the flames of eternal torment just for the sin of *not believing* in a God who hates Negroes and Chinese. Most of all, I hated the way Nebraskans, young and old, actually took smug pride in their own lack of sophistication. They wore their ingenuousness like a badge of honor, and rudely ridiculed and bullied anyone else who *did not* also proudly clothe themselves with the same course robe of premeditated ignorance.

I admit this must sound terribly unkind. Hate is a strong and unhealthy passion, especially for a nine year old boy. But hate springs from *fear* (real or imagined), and in my young mind there was much to fear in Nebraska. Even as a youngster I sensed a palpable darkness, a prairie madness, a nameless evil brooding just underneath the surface of the bib overalls and cotton house dresses; a slumbering beast just waiting to be awakened by the kiss of alcohol or jealousy or greed or lust; an evil that is ever mindful the nearest policeman is many miles (and perhaps hours) away; a black and primitive wickedness that takes poisonous root in the solitary psyche of those who toil alone in the earth from dawn to dusk, season-after-season, year-after-year; an evil that smothers in the heart all breath of human compassion or empathy for the pain and terror they inflict daily on the helpless beasts they breed for slaughter or the children they breed for labor and war; a twisted and perverse evil that feeds on guilt and self-loathing; an evil that incubates in the deafening silence of sweltering summer nights or the perpetual darkness of winter and hideously hatches like a basilisk egg into monstrous acts of rape and incest, and murder, and suicide.

The houses themselves are possessed of dark subconscious secrets—indeed, they are built upon them. Unlike the sunny and uninsulated bungalows of Southern California, Nebraska houses hide their own dungeons. Large as the footprint of the house itself, these cinder block chambers (the natives call them "basements") offer a modicum of insolation from the frozen sod of winter, and an area of damp coolness from the blistering heat of summer. Basements also provided residents a dark hole in the ground in which to cower from the whirling death clouds called tornados—tangible wind devils that regularly strike down from pus-green clouds and sweep across the earth bringing grotesque death and destruction to anything and everyone in their path.

Yes. There was much for a young man to fear in Nebraska. I was lonely, depressed, and morose. One sweltering humid summer morning I became so desperately bored I did something unthinkable for a nine year old boy in Nebraska.

I found something to read.

That morning I lingered in my sweat-soaked bed until I knew I was alone in the house. I got up and turned on our old Raytheon television set in the living room but could only get a scattered signal of a farm report. Like electricity and indoor toilets, television was new to rural Nebraska, and what few broadcast stations in operation were very far away. Reluctantly I switched off the crackling television and turned my attention to the living room bookcase. I looked for something—anything—that might alleviate my ennui or titillate my idle brain.

The family library had a few things that might distract me. My father was a pretty interesting guy (a native

Californian and very *un*-Nebraskan). He valued education, and wanted his sons to cherish books, so had recently purchased a new set of *World Book Encyclopedia* to display next to a few old sets of matched volumes of of literature. I figured the Encyclopedia would be too much like homework, so I turned my attention to an old 20 volume set of the *World's Greatest Literature.*[4]

At first glance *The Last of the Mohicans* looked like it might be fun but I soon discovered it much too grownup and difficult. I finally settled on *Volume 8* of the series, *Tales of Mystery and Imagination,* by Edgar Alan Poe. I opened it up and I saw to my delight that it was a collection of short stories that had titles that were absolutely irresistible to a miserable nine year old boy: *The Premature Burial, The Masque of the Red Death, The Tell-Tale Heart*, etc. Premature burials and red death sounded very promising indeed, but back in California I had actually seen a terrifying cartoon[5] called *The Tell-Tale Heart* at the old Lakewood Theater. I recalled at the time my mother became very upset with my older brother Marc for taking "little Lonnie" to see such an adult and disturbing film. I poured myself a glass of buttermilk, plopped down in the big chair by the open window and opened the book.

Once I started to read, however, I knew I was way out of my depth. There were lots of big words and incomprehensible foreign language phrases and epigrams, and geographic references. Every other sentence seem to make reference to some ancient legend or myth or classic poem. I was forced to actually *use* the dictionary

---

4   Spencer Press, 1936. He must have had the books since before he married Mom.

5   *The Tell-Tale Heart*. Columbia Pictures, 1953. Directed by Ted Parmelee, narrated by James Mason, screenplay by Bill Scott and Fred Grable.

and encyclopedia just to plod my way through the first story, *The Pit and the Pendulum*. But I eventually *did* get through it, and after I closed the book I realized I had become someone else—someone I liked—someone who could use the dictionary and encyclopedia; I learned about the horrors of the Spanish Inquisition (How delightfully evil was *that!*); I was exposed for the first time to the melodically elegant use of the English language;[6] most importantly, I discovered I was capable of being touched by art—capable of being possessed by *passion*. My ennui lifted and was replaced by a pre-adolescent worship of the macabre and the genius and wit of its creators. This passion has yet to subside. I spent the rest of that summer with Poe . . . and the dictionary, and the *World Book Encyclopedia*.

Ironically, the same 19th century-*esque* liabilities I despised about 1950s Nebraska life proved to be priceless assets of atmosphere that allowed me to conjure the perfect reading environment to savor the ecstasy of classic horror.

Horror takes its time, and to properly appreciate it you must also take your time. It has a pace, a slow, incessant rhythm—like your own heartbeat—like your own breath. After all, the great innovators of the art were writers of the Gilded Age who wrote for a 19th and early 20th century audience.[7] Nebraska in 1957 definitely had both her feet planted firmly in the 19th and early 20th centuries. That summer morning in 1957 could have just as easily been 1857, accompanied by the

---

6 I had to read Poe so deliberately that I felt as though I was reading aloud. In my soul, Poe's voice carried the gentlest lilt of a fine Southern gentleman and the tortured desperation of my favorite actor, Vincent Prince.

7 The offerings in this anthology date from 1851 to 1922.

same sound-track of bucolic silence; the same light searing through the same sun-stained yellow window shades; no hint of modern objective reality, no diversions of bustling civilization; no diversions of airplanes roaring overhead, no freeways in the distance, no sirens, no television, no radio, no air-conditioner; only the white noise of a million cicadas and the hiss of my own blood running through my brain, the incessant swing of the pendulum of an ancient clock, the barking of a distant dog, the cawing of a crow, the almost imperceptible whisper of the delicate film of curtains as they billow gently toward me like the gossamer negligée of a love-sick ghost.

This was the background music of my honeymoon with horror—playing as the honey-sweet words of Edgar Alan Poe, lugubriously wove elegant phrases from the age of gilded manners into a symphony of tortured rapture. Only had I been obliged to read the yellowing pages by the light of a whale oil lamp could my anachronistic reading experience been more exquisitely atmospheric.

I was so lucky.

Today most of us find it almost impossible to recapture the sepia-toned world that best conducts horror from the page to the soul. Twenty-first century readers, spoiled by spectacular special effects of the cinema, demand from the written word instant gratification, explosive shocks, and gore-splattered attacks upon the senses. We no longer allow ourselves time to refine the rapture of terror. We wolf down the junk-food snacks of violence and carnage when, with just a little patience, we could leisurely savor a rich and soul-satisfying banquet of elegant horror. We are missing so much.

That summer with Poe and my newly awakened love for the written word would eventually have profound effects upon my life; the most obvious being my eventual career as a writer. Writing is not only what I do for a living, it is my art, my joy, my voice, my meditation, my prayer, my confession, my declaration of independence, my act of worship, my song of self-awareness. My profession, however, has taken many years to evolve and develop. My 1957 boyhood love affair with horror had more immediate and dramatic consequences. Simply put—*I woke up*.

Poe's narrative voice clearly revealed to me that I possessed my own narrative voice. That hot, summer morning my consciousness instantly expanded. I no longer just passively *saw* or *heard* or *smelled* or *felt* the things around me. I woke up and became consciously *aware* that I was seeing and hearing and smelling and feeling the things around me. I became at once the observer and the observed of my own movie, and like the voice-over narration in a film-noir detective story I began to tell myself the bed-time story of my own existence, and the narration continues to this moment.

Thank you Edgar Alan Poe. Thank you horror literature.

The genre of classic horror has also changed the world. It can be argued that horror is the mother of science fiction—and that science fiction has molded the future and touched the consciousness of countless millions of fans who now have given themselves permission to dream like gods. In its way, horror is the grandmother of theoretical mathematics, quantum physics, and the mutation of intelligence in this corner of the galaxy. But it all had to start somewhere, and the editors of this anthology have labored lovingly to pay homage to the founding fathers of art form. Some of them, like Edgar Alan Poe or H.P. Lovecraft, or Bram Stoker, or Sir Arthur Conan Doyle require little or no introduction. But others are perhaps less familiar to you. We have provided the briefest of biographical sketches for all our authors at the beginning of each selections, but I would like to take this opportunity to write a few extra words about three of the stars of our production who also deserve, in my opinion to be recognized as *founding fathers* of horror:

Sir Edward Bulwer-Lytton, who I believe should be credited with establishing early in the 19th century the archetypal form and devices of the horror genre;

Robert W. Chambers, who late in the 19th century broke the space-time membrane of gothic horror and smashed open the doors of our subconscious—the same doors from which H. P. Lovecraft's primordial "Old Ones" would ooze out forcing us to cower before our shadow souls;

and Aleister Crowley, a real-life, unapologetic black magician who early in the 20th century rolled up his sleeves and did battle with those shadows to turn demons of darkness into angels of light.

Sir Edward Bulwer-Lytton (1803-1873)

Have you ever heard the phrases?

"It was a dark and stormy night . . . ." or,

"The pen is mightier than the sword . . . ." or,

"Pursuit of the almighty dollar."

These familiar clichés first poured forth from the pen of Sir Edward Bulwer-Lytton the prolific English playwright, poet and novelist. As might be expected of a gentleman of his breeding, the noble Lord Lytton pursued these literary diversions as an amateur while he busied himself with the serious duties of serving his Queen (Victoria) as *Secretary of State for the Colonies* and a wide assortment of other stiff-collared diplomatic and political responsibilities. He published his first book of poems in 1820, and in 1828, when his semi-titillating essay on the whimsical subject of nineteenth century *dandyism* was released, it was clear to the reading public that here was a fellow who could be wryly entertaining as well as erudite.

While his occult tales and horror stories have become favorites of lovers of the mysterious and macabre, Lytton's most publically beloved and familiar works remain his post-biblical epic, *The Last Days of Pompeii* (1834) which has over the years captured the imagination of film makers; and his dramatic historical fiction, *Rienzi* (1835) which Richard Wagner turned into an enduring opera. His popularity with the general public notwithstanding, Lord Lytton deserves serious recognition as one of the primary godfathers of horror. This enduring admiration attests to his skill with words, but even more impressive are his impeccable credentials among serious occultists.

Although empirical evidence is absent, Lytton is said to have been an initiate of one or more of the mysterious continental magical secret societies that obliquely claimed they were of ancient Rosicrucian origins. He was almost certainly the friend and confidant of the great French magician, Alphonse Louis Constant (Eliphas Levi, 1810–1875), the father of modern ceremonial magic.

As a young member of the Rosicrucian Order, AMORC, I was instructed by my elder adepts (in no uncertain terms) that I was to read and study the *works of Lord Lytton*, especially his occult story "Zanoni."[8] Written in 1842 (a full generation before the founding of Madam Blavatsky's *Theosophical Society* or the *Hermetic Order of the Golden Dawn*) the opening words of Zanoni can be interpreted as a Rosicrucian confession from Lord Lytton himself:

> It so chanced that some years ago, in my younger days, whether of authorship of life, I felt the desire to make myself acquainted with the true origins and tenets of the singular sect known by the name of Rosicrucians.[9]

While the plot of Zanoni is a darkly appealing love story that inaugurates all the genteel devices of classic horror-love that we will (a few years later) recognize in the works of Edgar Alan Poe, Robert W. Chambers, and others. But the text of Zanoni also reveals (to the trained eye) the language of a fellow occultist. In fact, it is clear that Zanoni could not possibly have been written by anyone other than a *bona fide* initiate of the mysteries. The story even makes indirect references to a magic *book*—a book that is undoubtedly the very *real* tome known to scholars today as *The Book of Abra-Melin*.[10] This landmark occult grimoire (c. 1378) would

---

8   See *Zanoni,* Books 1, 2, and 3, San Francisco, Newburyport, Massachusetts: Weiser Books, 2012.

9   See *Zanoni,* Books 1, 2, and 3, San Francisco, Newburyport, Massachusetts: Weiser Books, 2012.

10 *The Book of Abramelin.* Abraham Von Worms. Georg Dehn, Ed., Steven Guth, tras., foreword by Lon Milo DuQuette. Lake Worth, Florida Nicholas Hays, Inc. 2006.

remain untranslated and unknown to the English-speaking world (or indeed anyone but the most knowledgeable and serious student of the occult) until 1888 when Golden Dawn adept S. L. MacGreggor Mathers translated fragments of the text which he found in the Bibliotheque de l'Arsenal in Paris.

The Book of Abra-Melin is considered by many to be the Rosetta stone of Western Magick, elevating the misunderstood superstations of the mediaeval sorcerers to a spiritual science as sacred and viable as the self-transformational traditions of eastern mysticism. As it would seem, His Lordship, Sir Edward Bulwer-Lytton—dandy, diplomat, and novelist—was rubbing elbows on a regular basis with very same mystics and magicians who not only knew of the book's existence but were intimately familiar with its contents and significance.

It is clear to me that where secret occult mysteries and practices are concerned it was not a case of Lord Lytton gleaning his occult knowledge from 19th century English Rosicrucian pretenders, but one of 19th century "Rosicrucians" getting their occult knowledge from *him*!

While we heap praise on Lytton for being a founding father of *horror*, we must also credit him for helping introduce the world to the genre of *science fiction*. His 1871 novel, *The Coming Race* would prove to be a breathtaking and disturbing look into the future. Unfortunately, early in the 20th century the imaginative ideas put forth in *The Coming Race* would be seized and distorted into a monstrous vision by the madmen of Germany's Third Reich, and employed like some malevolent conjuration to invoke a great demon upon the earth in the form of the genocidal terrors of the

Second World War. No horror fiction story can possibly compare to such unimaginable evil—such incalculable pain and death suffered by millions-upon-millions of our fellow human beings.

Of course, I am not suggesting we should blame Lord Edward Bulwer-Lytton for the genocidal horror of the holocaust. However, we would all do well to be mindful of Lytton's own words, "The pen is mightier than the sword." and be mindful of the awesome power the written word has to effect changes in human consciousness either for for good or for ill.

Robert W. Chambers (1827–1911)

If H.P. Lovecraft is the *Christ of Horror*, then most assuredly Robert W. Chambers was his *John the Baptist*.

Recently it was my privilege to introduce and curate the series of short stories first published in 1895 under the collective tile: *The King in Yellow*, by Robert W. Chambers.[11] To avoid paraphrasing myself I append a portion of my introduction below. While I refer specifically to *The King in Yellow*, my observations of Chambers' style, technique and imagination apply also to our Chambers selection, *The Messenger*.

Perhaps you have heard of *The King in Yellow*? No? Neither had I until a few years ago when a film maker contacted me and informed me he was making a film of *The King in Yellow*, and asked if I would be interested in appearing in a cameo role in his production. Before I gave him my answer (the project was later abandoned) I did a bit of digging and discovered a most remarkable

---

11 See excerpts from the *The King in Yellow*, by Robert W. Chambers, in *Yellow Sign*, *The Mask*, *The Demoiselle D'ys*, and *In the Court of the Dragon*, introduced by Lon Milo DuQuette, Newburyport, Massachusetts: Weiser Books, 2012.

treasure—a terrifying work of American *horror* that predates by a quarter century the first short story by H. P. Lovecraft. Indeed, *The King in Yellow*, by Robert W. Chambers, is arguably the archetypal inspiration for what would become an entire genre of horror-fiction for which the immortal Lovecraft is ultimately credited.

Robert W. Chambers (1865–1933) is not exactly a household name; but that has not always been the case. Late in his career his romantic novels and historical fictions were wildly popular, his books bestsellers, his magazine installments eagerly awaited. For a time he was considered the most successful American literary figure of the day. Yet his later and lighter offerings, while bringing him fame and modest fortune, are forgettable *bonbons* when compared to the strong meat and innovative brilliance of his horror fiction. The most notable of all his work is *The King in Yellow*, a collection of short stories whose plots are loosely connected to an infamous imaginary book and play of the same title banned universally because of its ominous tendency to drive mad those who read it or came in contact with it. Indeed, the terror begins immediately with the reader unsure whether or not madness and suicide will be the price he or she will pay for turning the page.

I was a bit disoriented when I began reading *The King in Yellow's* opening story—a dizzying effect that I'm sure Chambers intended to induce in the minds of his "gay-nineties" readers. The tale, called "The Repairer of Reputations," takes place in the science fiction "future" of a 1920's New York City, a metropolis of street names, parks and landmarks familiar to us still today which Chambers meticulously paints from his rich palette of images (he was, after all, a classically trained and skilled artist and designer). However, there is something disturbingly tweaked with the entire milieu of the story. It all takes place in a utopian and prosperous post-civil war America—a blend of aristocratic republic and military dictatorship that could have easily evolved from the strange bed-fellows of the gilded age's contending movements: nationalistic laissez faire capitalism and the liberal yet pragmatic ideals of social progressivism. From the opening lines, we are instantly plunged into an alternate reality where the comfortable and familiar past has been slightly altered and we are forced to confront the infinite "what ifs" of history and in doing so calling into question the objective reality of the present.

Nestled within this surreal environment we are introduced to a well-spoken narrator who at first seems to be a faithful servant of the truth but who will soon give us reason to doubt both his sanity and our own. But I won't spoil that for you.

Like Lovecraft would do decades later, Chambers allows the reader's own imagination to do the heavy lifting of terror. Cassilda's Song which serves as the epigram for the entire work is supposedly clipped from Act I, Scene 2 of the play, *The King in Yellow*, and without burdening the reader's imagination with concrete certitudes conjures images of strange locales and vistas not of this earth, indeed, not of this universe, and only hints of characters of unspeakable power and horror.

Along the shore the cloud waves break,
The twin suns sink beneath the lake,
The shadows lengthen
In Carcosa.

Strange is the night where black stars rise,
And strange moons circle through the skies
But stranger still is
Lost Carcosa.

Songs that the Hyades shall sing,
Where flap the tatters of the King,
Must die unheard in
Dim Carcosa.

Song of my soul, my voice is dead,
Die thou, unsung, as tears unshed
Shall dry and die in
Lost Carcosa.

Like all great works of horror, the story becomes disturbing, dark and terrifying in direct proportion to the degree to which our own hearts and minds are disturbed, dark and frightened.

Aleister Crowley (1875–1947)

Unlike Lord Lytton and Robert Chambers, Aleister Crowley is *not* remembered primarily for his works of fiction. Admittedly, he was a prolific poet, and in this capacity, even in his early twenties, he received a measure of critical praise and encouragement. His two novels, *Moonchild* (1917), and *Diary of a Drug Fiend* (1922) also received a modicum of critical recognition and over the years have indirectly inspired a handful of film efforts.

His short stories,[12] plays, and essays (most privately published and now treasures coveted by collectors) were obviously written for an elite audience of highly educated esotericists and close associates capable of appreciating his elaborate in-jokes, pornographic allusions, and obscure references. As much as he lamented his rejection by the public it appears he went to great lengths to openly court his own vilification.

For the reader who is completely unfamiliar with the person of Aleister Crowley I highly recommend his own *Confessions*[13] and the recent biography, *Perdurabo— The Life of Aleister Crowley.*[14] I has been my pleasure and challenge to write a handful of books concerning the life and work of this remarkable man. The following brief excerpt is from my book, *Understanding Aleister Crowley's Thoth Tarot*[15].

Paradoxes seem to define the life and career of Edward Alexander (Aleister) Crowley.[16] Yes, in many ways he was a scoundrel. There is no doubt that he wallowed shamelessly in his carefully cultivated persona as England's literary and spiritual bad-boy. At the same time he took life and himself very seriously. Among other distinctions, he was a world-class mountaineer,[17] chess master, painter, poet, sportsman, novelist, critic, and theatrical

---

12 Including *The Testament of Magdalen Blair*, which appears in this anthology.
13 *The Confessions of Aleister Crowley*, London, 1929. Abridged one-volume edition, ed John Symonds and Kenneth Grant. London, 1969; reprint, London and New York: Arkana, 1989.
14 *Perdurabo: The Life of Aleister Crowley,* by Richard Kaczynski, PhD, Berkeley: North Atlantic Books, 2010.
15 *Understanding Aleister Crowley's Thoth Tarot*, by Lon Milo DuQuette, (York Beach, Maine: Red Wheel/Weiser, 2003), pp 7-8.
16 1875–1947.
17 By 1920 Crowley still held the world's record for a number of mountaineering feats including the greatest pace uphill (4,000 feet in 83 minutes) at over 16,000 feet on Mexico's Iztaccihuatl in 1900; the first ascent of the Nevado de Toluca by a solitary climber 1901; and his 1902 assault on K2 where he spent 65 days on the Baltoro glacier.

producer. He introduced America to Astrology,[18] Isadora Duncan to the *I Ching*, Aldous Huxley to mescaline, and the poet Victor Neuberg to hiking and high magick. As an *agent provocateur*, writing for an English-language German propaganda newspaper in New York, he penned the outrageous and inflammatory editorials that provoked a reluctant United States Congress to enter the First World War on England's side.[19]

During the Second World War, at the request of friend and Naval Intelligence officer Ian Fleming,[20] Crowley provided Winston Churchill with valuable insights into the superstitions and magical mind-set of the leaders of the Third Reich. He also suggested to the Prime Minister, if reports can be believed, that he exploit the enemy's magical paranoia by being photographed as much as possible giving the two-fingered "V for Victory" gesture. This sign is the manual version of the magical sign of Apophis-Typhon, a powerful symbol of destruction and annihilation, that, according

---

18 Ghostwriting for Evangeline Adams, Crowley wrote the bulk of the material first published under her name, including her classic texts, *Astrology: Your Place in the Sun* (1927) and *Astrology: Your Place Among the Stars* (1930). These works made "Astrology" a household word in America and Europe and catapulted Adams to celebrated status as "Astrologer to Wall Street and Washington." Recently Crowley's co-authorship has been graciously acknowledged by the Adams estate and has resulted in the release of *The General Principles of Astrology* by Aleister Crowley and Evangeline Adams, York Beach, Maine: Red Wheel/ Weiser, 2001.

19 It is often forgotten that the United States was very close to entering the First World War on *Germany's* side. Much to the horror of the German Foreign Ministry, Crowley's editorials made it appear that it was Germany's intention (in fact its foreign policy) to engage in unrestricted submarine warfare against civilian shipping. Even though this was at the time an outrageous falsehood, Crowley's editorials were used to create an anti-German hysteria that would eventually sweep the United States into the conflict on England's side. In a very real way, Aleister Crowley saved his beloved England using only his pen as a magical wand.

20 Ian (Lancaster) Fleming (1908–1964)—pseudonym, Atticus—British journalist, secret service agent, writer, whose most famous creation was superhero James Bond, Agent 007. Crowley and Fleming were indeed friends. Copies of their correspondence still exist, some of which discuss matters of occult propaganda and the interrogation of Rudolf Hess.

to magical tradition is capable of defeating the solar energies represented by the swastika.

Astonishingly, Crowley's adventures and achievements, more than any dozen men of ambition and genius could realistically hope to garner in a lifetime, seem almost to be distractions when weighed against his monumental exploits of self-discovery. His visionary writings and his efforts to synthesize and integrate esoteric spiritual systems of East and West[21] make him one of the most fascinating cultural and religious figures of the 20th Century.

Even though Crowley did not, like Edward Bulwer-Lytton, invent the genre that would define the format and atmosphere of classic horror; even though he wasn't responsible for transforming horror into the morbid-sweet love-song of a tormented soul like Edgar Alan Poe; even though he didn't smash the dimensional boundaries of space-time to plumb new depths of psychological hell like Robert Chambers and H. P. Lovecraft; he did something none of them did. He actually lived the terrifying and ecstatic events of the real life horror-love story-adventure of his own amazing life.

Crowley is not important to us for the horror stories he *wrote*—but for the magnificent horror story he *was*.

He didn't just write about demons, and devils, and angels, vampires, he invoked them, evoked them, conjured them, battled them, conquered them; He didn't just write about the wonders and terrors of other dimensions, he willfully penetrated them, navigated them, transcended them—*then* he wrote about them in exacting detail.

---

21 He called his system "Scientific Illuminism"—Its motto: "The Method of Science—The Aim of Religion."

Nearly seventy years after his death, the man who the tabloids called the "most dangerous man on earth," the man they called the "wickedest man in the world," the man who in all seriousness called *himself* the "Beast 666" is now receiving the academic and philosophical attention and recognition that eluded him in life.

Crowley's influence today on the literary art form of horror is incalculable. There isn't a modern writer of horror, science fiction or fantasy who has not in some fundamental way been directly or indirectly influenced by Crowley.

Crowley's dead. But his horror reaches from beyond the grave. Robert Chambers wrote of an accursed book and play called *The King in Yellow*. Supposedly, everyone who read *The King in Yellow* went hideously insane. I think of that and smile when I encounter people today who still fearfully hold the person of Aleister Crowley in superstitious awe.

"Is it dangerous to study Aleister Crowley?" I am still asked.

Aleister Crowley was by no means perfect. He was not good with people, and often alienated those who loved him dearest. His bold explorations of human sexuality and drugs (always meticulously recorded and analyzed) are fascinating to study, but were never intended to be casually emulated. I have never encountered anyone who knew him that did not disapprove of some aspect of his character or behavior.

But he is dead. For us, only his works remain as a measure of the man, and they are currently more accessible to the general public than at any time during his life. His influence on the modern world of art, literature, religion, and philosophy is now widely acknowledged even by his most vehement critics. . . .

But, is it dangerous for some people to study Aleister Crowley? I guess I have to say "Yes." For those whose belief in a God of goodness hinges upon the reality of Devil who is equally evil—for the superstitious, the ignorant, the lazy, the immature, the unbalanced, the mentally ill, the paranoid, the faint-hearted; for anyone who for any reason cannot or will not take responsibility for their own actions, their own lives, their own souls; for these people Aleister Crowley is still a very dangerous man.[22]

And now dear reader I will leave you to enjoy the works of these three masters of horror and the choir of other luminaries of the genre. I sincerely hope you enjoy your time with them and will treasure this beautifully produced book. Perhaps when you have finished reading it you'll want to put it in your family library— near the dictionary and encyclopedia. Who knows, perhaps someday some bored young man or woman will discover it on a hot summer morning.

For the time being . . . I bid you goodnight.

---

22 From *The Magick of Aleister Crowley*. Lon Milo DuQuette, Newburyport, Massachusetts: Weiser Books. 2003, p. 8.

ABOUT THE AUTHOR

In the dark and brooding firmament of occult literature, Lon Milo DuQuette is a star of unique and exceptional brilliance who has earned the distinction of being able to make complex magical and spiritual concepts amusing, entertaining, and easily digestible. This rare combination of scholarship and self-effacing humor has in the last thirty years secured him a unique and respected position in the world of esoteric literature. He is an internationally recognized authority on Ceremonial Magick, Qabalah, Tarot, and the life and teachings of noted English occultist Aleister Crowley (1875–1947). DuQuette has authored seventeen books (translated into twelve languages), including *The Chicken Qabalah of Rabbi Lamed Ben Clifford* and *Understanding Aleister Crowley's Thoth Tarot*. His passion for writing is not limited to his magick. He is also an award-winning singer-songwriter and recording artist whose musical career has spanned over fifty years.

Since 1975, DuQuette has served as an administrative officer of *Ordo Templi Orientis* (O.T.O.), one of the most influential and controversial magical societies of the 20th (now 21st) century. He is an acknowledged authority on the life and works of Aleister Crowley (the 100-year-old organization's most celebrated and notorious leader). Since 1994, he has served as the O.T.O.'s United States Deputy National Grand Master. He travels extensively each year to lecture, teach, and perform his music. He is arguably the Order's most visible representative.

Born in Long Beach, California, in 1948, he moved as a child to Columbus, Nebraska, where he would meet his wife-to-be, Constance (his high-school sweetheart). Moving back to California the moment he graduated from high school, Lon promptly proposed to Constance over the telephone (under the mystical inspiration of LSD). They were married in 1967 and have remained magickal partners ever since. (This is an accomplishment Lon considers his greatest magical achievement.) They have one son, Dr. Jean-Paul DuQuette of Macau, China.

TO OUR READERS

Weiser Books, an imprint of Red Wheel/Weiser, publishes books across the entire spectrum of occult, esoteric, speculative, and New Age subjects. Our mission is to publish quality books that will make a difference in people's lives without advocating any one particular path or field of study. We value the integrity, originality, and depth of knowledge of our authors.

Our readers are our most important resource, and we appreciate your input, suggestions, and ideas about what you would like to see published.

Visit our website at *www.redwheelweiser.com* to learn about our upcoming books and free downloads, and be sure to go to *www.redwheelweiser.com/newsletter* to sign up for newsletters and exclusive offers.

You can also contact us at *info@rwwbooks.com* or at

Red Wheel/Weiser, LLC
65 Parker Street, Suite 7
Newburyport, MA 01950